AgendaMusica

Richard Payne

If found, please return to:

_____

_____

_____

_____

_____

Table of Contents

Quick start guide

Start with your musical ambitions. What are they? Think deeply about what you'd like to be able to accomplish musically. Use pages 12 to 15 to brainstorm and organize your goals.

Next, map a course to your goals by connecting each of them to specific skills, exercises, and tasks. It's great if you can work with a teacher, but not impossible to create a plan for yourself, either on your own or with the help of other musicians you know or watch online. Some ideas and suggestions appear across the bottom of pages 12 to 15.

Jump into the Weekly Practice Journal. Each practice week consists of two pages: a right-hand page with your practice task list, and a left-hand page with reflection questions and space for notes. Practice Week 1 begins on page 16.

Then, practice. As you complete your various tasks, mark the days on which you did them, rate the quality of your practice session, and record the time you spent practicing.

As you go along your week, reflect on the qualitative aspects of your practice. Write brief reactions to your listening assignments. Note things you want to work on or be more mindful about. Write down any questions that arise. Journal your thoughts and self-criticisms.

At the end of each practice week, complete the Weekly Check-in section to record what most inspired you, what went well, and what went less well. Write a simple thought or idea to keep in mind and encourage and motivate you for the week to come. Finally, rate your overall satisfaction with the practice quality of your week's sessions.

Then, to help you visualize the big picture of your practice, transfer to the Progress Charts that begin on page 68 your total weekly practice time, daily average practice time, and overall practice satisfaction rating. Use the extra space provided to add other graphic representations of progress that you'd find helpful.

At the end of six months of practice, reflect on the experience and consider your path forward by answering the questions on pages 90 and 91. Use your insights to guide your subsequent six months with a new copy of AgendaMusica.

Finally, keeping track of your repertoire and reminding yourself to practice it is an important task for every musician. The last page, 92, is a place in which you can list all of the pieces you've learned over the past 26 weeks and track when each has been practiced.

That's the overview. Before embarking on your musical journey, read the specific details and suggestions on how to use each component of AgendaMusica on the pages immediately following.

How to plan, focus, and track your music practice

First things first: mastering any skill takes discipline. And time. And increasingly complex and sophisticated thought. Among other things.

Music is no different. Listen to any of the master musicians talk about their craft. They work hard and think deeply about their music and their playing.

AgendaMusica can help you cultivate that discipline and depth of thought. It challenges you to think reflectively about your playing and musical development.

Some may welcome and embrace the structure and breadth. If that's you, dive right in!

Others may find the full program a little daunting. That's ok. Start slowly. Focus on getting your weekly assignments down and any additional components you find interesting or provocative. Then add components whenever you're ready and try to work your way up to the full program.

Overview

Start with a clear understanding of your musical goals. Then connect specific practice elements to those goals to keep yourself motivated and on your chosen path.

Next, practice those particular and intentional elements consistently to move yourself ever forward. Monitor continuously to reward your efforts and steadfastness and to document your journey for future reference and contemplation.

Reflect deeply and regularly to fine-tune your program and to discover indispensable personal insights. Finally, chart and analyze your progress to capture the big picture of your labors and to reinforce your persistence and commitment.

AgendaMusica is an approach to practice that keeps all of the physical and mental components of good musical practice front and center in your awareness. The result is more intentional and mindful musical growth and performance.

Goal setting

When beginning any learning program, including musical development, an important first step is to identify your goals. Each of your goals is probably associated with a time by which you'd like to complete it. Some you might want to accomplish today, some within a week or a month, some within six months or a year, some in two, five, or ten years, or even longer.

Although it can be tremendously motivating to state on the goal-setting page what you'd like to achieve in the very long term, consider using the space primarily to identify your mid-range goals, or those you'd like to accomplish in the next six months to one year.

So: brainstorm. Write down whatever you presently want to achieve. Don't mentally edit or judge your ideas. Don't omit something important to you just because you're not sure how you might accomplish it. Just use the space to identify what end results or accomplishments would be most meaningful to you.

GOALS
- Improvise against a basic chord progression
- Sight-read melodies from the Real Book
- Learn inversions for sevenths and ninths
- Learn 5 songs well enough to play for others
- Find other musicians to play music with

Try to be as specific as possible. Instead of saying generally that you aspire to be a "great trumpeter," try to express the evidence of such greatness. What does being a great trumpeter look like to you personally? Maybe it's being able to play well a particularly complex piece. Maybe it's a successful audition. It could be anything, as long as it matters to you and you can measure whether or not it's happened.

Coming up with goals is often a very personal matter. However, it may also help to explore or refine your goals with your music teacher or someone else who knows you and whom you trust.

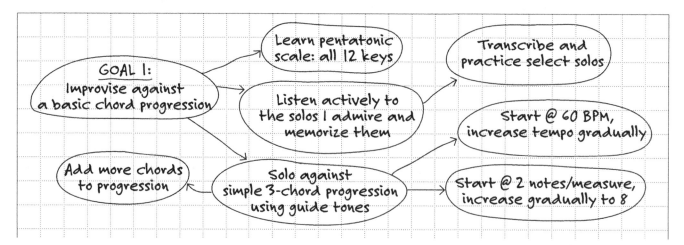

You can write your goals in list form (that is, a series of statements that you go back and number to indicate the relative importance of each). Or perhaps try mind-map style (that is, enclose each written goal in its own circle and use the size of the circles to indicate each goal's relative importance. In the ideation stage, strive for as complete a list as you can. No one else needs to see your list, so don't judge or censor yourself.

Once you are confident that you've gotten on paper all you'd like to accomplish, it's time to prioritize. Select the three to five goals that you're reasonably confident could be accomplished in the next six months to one year. Underline them. Color them in red. Do something to make them stand out.

(Don't worry. You won't toss out everything else you want to accomplish, it's just that taking action on too many goals can be overwhelming, dispiriting, and dividing of your practicing attention. And if you've identified your goals well, you'll probably not only improve your skills in the areas you've prioritized but will also make at least some progress in areas not in your present focus.)

To give you a more precise practicing roadmap, identify the subtasks you'll need to work on to be able to achieve each of your three to five prioritized goals. A music teacher is probably best able to break down the specific components you'll need to work on. But your own research, intuition, or a peer's insights and experiences might also suggest how to get from where you are to where you want to be.

To help you connect your goals with practice sessions, the bottom of the goal-setting page has some suggestions of general skills and topics that might serve as a starting place. So, let's say you want to improve your ability to improvise. If you're a beginner, you might want to work on scales and listening. If you're more advanced, you might want to work on transcribing the solos of others and improvising against basic progressions.

The goal of goal setting is to translate your vague, abstract, and future aspirations into actions that are more specific and concrete and present-focused. Only when you see the clear connection between what you're practicing and where it's going to take you will you be able to summon the energy and enthusiasm that keeps you practicing. You'll keep the big picture in mind.

Remembering and revisiting your goals may be all you need to motivate you to practice in the face of the inevitable times when you're too tired, too busy, or too whatever-excuse to pick up your instrument and play.

Weekly Practice Journal

So, what exactly should you practice? Too often, there's a tendency to rely on memory or mood or inertia or simplicity or some other random or spur-of-the-moment whim. Of course, any of those strategies are better than not practicing at all. But none are really systematic enough to maximize ongoing musical growth. That's simply because we tend easily to forget.

To practice systematically, you have to write down on paper what you should be practicing.

Writing down specific tasks keeps practice structured and unambiguous. If you want to give yourself maximal structure, add a target number of repetitions or the number of minutes you need to practice an exercise before you can count it as having been completed.

When forming new practicing habits, it's important to reward yourself as you go along. So, once you complete a task, put a simple check mark in the circle of that day's column. You'll be surprised how reinforcing a string of check marks for completed tasks across a week can be.

Of course, if you only want to practice a task on certain days, make a mark of your choosing to identify those days: draw a square around that day's completion circle, highlight it in some way, or darken the squares of days that you don't want to practice that task. And, of course, check each corresponding circle when the task is completed.

When the week's practice is written in advance, it minimizes the tendency to conveniently forget what one really should be practicing. Or to get distracted by the more familiar, well-rehearsed, and fun things to play.

Or to avoid a particular task or two because of anxiety or perfectionism—that is, when an exercise's challenge is skipped because it's seen as intimidating or unfamiliar or uncomfortable despite knowing its important contribution to growth.

There are seven general activities to consider incorporating into every musician's practice routine: warming-up and preparing to play; putting yourself into a practicing mindset; practicing fundamentals and drills; focusing to develop or master one specific piece, area, topic, skill, or technique; rehearsing your repertoire; listening to others and yourself; and reflecting on your performance and progress.

Each week has two pages to help you capture those general activities. One on the right-hand side on which to identify your practice assignments. And one on the left-hand side on which to record reactions to your listening and to reflect on your practice experience during the week.

The Assignments page

Set up the page by writing the week's starting date in the space in the upper left and right, along with writing in the corresponding days of the week in the columns. Then write goal-directed tasks for the week in each of the sections.

Some form of warm-up should probably come first, so it appears as the first section of the Weekly Practice Journal. However, practice the other elements in whatever order makes the most sense to you in your session. Number your preferred order if you like. Or skip around. Even change the order from day to day.

Warm-up exercises are important to prepare you to play physically and mentally. Warming up can also help avoid injury. Of course, warming up involves easing into playing with exercises that begin to get the blood flowing and muscles engaged in the more demanding work to come. However, the transition from the non-practicing to the practicing state might also involve a mindful acknowledgment of the shift in activity, stretching and breathing exercises, or attention to posture.

You can also warm up mentally and put yourself in a practicing mindset by spending some time exploring, improvising, and discovering how you can get the most out of your musical creativity and your instrument. The second section of the assignments page encourages you to include unstructured experimentation. For example, spend some time playing a wide range of musical dynamics in a free fashion, such as soft to loud, slow to fast, busy to spacious. Play around with one or two elements of your normal technique, such as standing on one leg or playing in a pitch-black room or using only two fingers or improvising with only four random notes. Play an emotion or a color or an animal. Play a story or a scene you recently observed. Or just play freely to see what sounds you can produce without worrying about scale or structure. Exercise your right-brain. Experiment, record, and reflect.

Drills are often the most dreaded part of a practice session. Yet some skills are so fundamental to playing that they must be learned by plain-and-simple memorization and mechanical

Date: **March 15, 2021**

		Day of the week	M	T	W	Th	F	S	Su

Warm-up / Preparation

		M	T	W	Th	F	S	Su
Stretching: shoulder and head rolls	10 reps/**mins**	✓	✓	✓	○	✓	✓	✓
Visualization: good posture, deep breathing, precision movements	2 reps/**mins**	✓	✓	✓	○	○	✓	✓
Harmonic minor scales, 3 octaves, both hands: A, E, B	5 reps/**mins**	✓	✓	✓	✓	○	✓	✓
	reps/mins	○	○	○	○	○	○	○
	reps/mins	○	○	○	○	○	○	○

Exploration / Improvisation / Discovery

		M	T	W	Th	F	S	Su
Play around with dynamics: soft to loud, slow to fast, busy to spacious	5 **mins**	○	✓	✓	○	○	✓	✓
Improvise over Major ii-V-I using only 4 notes	5 **mins**	✓	○	○	✓	○	○	✓
	mins	○	○	○	○	○	○	○

Fundamentals / Drills

		M	T	W	Th	F	S	Su
Hanon Exercise No. 5	5 reps/**mins**	○	✓	✓	✓	○	✓	✓
Cadences, 12 keys: I-VI-II-V-I	5 reps/**mins**	✓	✓	✓	○	○	✓	✓
Sight-read random page from Real Book	10 reps/**mins**	✓	✓	✓	○	✓	✓	✓
Practice new lick in all 12 keys	10 reps/mins	○	○	✓	○	✓	○	○
	reps/mins	○	○	○	○	○	○	○
	reps/mins	○	○	○	○	○	○	○
	reps/mins	○	○	○	○	○	○	○

Week's Focus *IMPROVISATION*

		M	T	W	Th	F	S	Su
Try to replicate Wynton Kelly's sound on Freddie Freeloader	10 reps/**mins**	○	✓	✓	○	✓	✓	✓
Solo over Donna Lee with constant stream of eighth notes	10 reps/**mins**	✓	✓	✓	✓	○	✓	✓
Begin transcribing Erroll Garner's solo: I'll Remember April	reps/mins	○	✓	○	○	○	✓	✓
	reps/mins	○	○	○	○	○	○	○
	reps/mins	○	○	○	○	○	○	○
	reps/mins	○	○	○	○	○	○	○
	reps/mins	○	○	○	○	○	○	○

Repertoire / Review / Rehearsal

		M	T	W	Th	F	S	Su
Practice Autumn Leaves: dynamics and moving bass	10 reps/**mins**	✓	✓	✓	○	✓	✓	✓
Practice My Shining Hour solo: attend to accents and attack	10 reps/**mins**	○	✓	✓	○	✓	✓	✓
(Record, listen back, note sections needing improvement, re-record!)	reps/mins	○	○	○	○	○	○	○
	reps/mins	○	○	○	○	○	○	○
	reps/mins	○	○	○	○	○	○	○

Daily Summary

	M	T	W	Th	F	S	Su
Practice session quality (rate ☺,☺,☹)	—	∪	∪	∩	∩	∪	∪
Length of day's practice session (mins)	55	82	90	25	50	125	110
Summary of week's practice time (mins)	537 Total / 7 Days = 77 Average						

repetition. For example, note identification. The circle of fifths and corresponding key signatures. Scales and modes in all of their color and richness. Chords and arpeggios. Intonation. Vibrato. Solfège. And so on. Accomplished players, regardless of instrument and musical style, know and maintain certain fundamental proficiencies by rote such that they become automatic and second nature.

Often the resistance to drills and other more rote fundamentals comes from not having a clear idea of why a particular exercise matters to your musical growth. So, if you find yourself bored or unwilling or even defiant in the face of drills, challenge yourself to do some research and understand exactly why a particular drill or rote exercise is important for you, and likely has been considered important by the masters. Ask your teacher or a fellow musician. Do an online search. Knowing why you're doing something will help you practice more mindfully and with greater enthusiasm and intent.

A central or primary focus for the week moves your musical development forward along a deliberate and purposeful path. Maybe this portion of your practice concentrates on something concrete, such as learning a specific song or composing a new piece. Perhaps the focus is more conceptual, such as paying attention to dynamics or intonation. Maybe it's theoretical, such as studying secondary dominant chords as a way to add harmonic tension. Regardless, your central focus provides a creative complement to rote learning's foundational skills.

Repertoire practice helps you to maintain proficiency with previously learned pieces or to master particular skills, such as improvising against a song or chord progression. More than likely, you spent significant time and energy learning new material. Unfortunately, without occasional if not frequent practice much of what's been learned will slowly wither from memory. Keep your favorites fresh by devoting a portion of your practice session to their preservation.

At the end of each practice day, rate the quality of your practice session in its Daily Summary section. If you choose to monitor the time you spent

practicing, enter that in the space provided and calculate a weekly average at week's end. Recording how much time you spent each day and over the course of the week can be a powerful psychological reinforcement that encourages regular practice.

The Reflection page

Listening, most professional musicians would agree, is an essential part of developing one's ear, one's style and technique of playing, and one's understanding and appreciation of music. And it is often overlooked or given short shrift. Indeed, listen to others. But also record and listen to yourself. Of course, listening needn't be limited to audio-only performances. It should certainly include video, whether of actual performances or of instruction or lectures or presentations on music theory, history, or any other topic that's relevant to your musical advancement. And don't forget to "listen" to what musicians, their biographers, their critics, and academics have to say in their many books, articles, and online posts.

The section for listening, watching, and reading notes gives you a place in which to record your brief impressions of particular musical pieces you've heard. (There are pages at the end of AgendaMusica for writing longer listening notes.)

During your reflection, ask yourself questions. For example, what was the mood of the piece? How did the piece make you feel? What images or emotions did it evoke? Where in particular did it succeed? Where did it fail? What might you take away from the piece and incorporate into your own approach to music? What one thing about the piece do you most want to remember? Write it down no matter how briefly. Then, over time, refer back to what you wrote and certainly appreciate those thoughts of yours that would have otherwise been lost to fallible memory.

Also take notes here on things you've read. A musician's thought-provoking approach to performance or composition. An interesting music-related news story, song history, or biographical fact that you found online. The key points from a presentation on some aspect of music theory. Perhaps tips on how to promote, market, or monetize your music. Or perhaps a particularly striking or inspirational quote you want to remember.

During the week, but especially at its end, take time to capture your personal thoughts about what you want to work on or be more mindful about. It could be something simple: watching your posture, taking a 20-minute break between range exercises, tapping your foot to maintain rhythm, not tapping your foot to internalize rhythm. You may want to remind yourself to watch your dynamics in measures 12 to 18, or to remember to use guide tones when improvising. It could be something you're considering adding to next week's practice. Or it might be something deeply personal and philosophical that you want to keep in mind to guide how you play or express yourself musically. (If you have a teacher, your teacher might want to use the space to write things for you to keep in mind or watch out for.)

Whatever it is, commit to writing it on paper. You see, our thoughts are so momentary and fleeting. Unless you freeze them on the page for future reference, you may certainly forget an idea that might be useful or provocative or inspirational in the future, whether next week, next year, or even many years from now.

And journaling your thoughts, that is to say, actually engaging in the sometimes-difficult process of finding the exact words, can help organize your thinking. Writing isn't easy. But writing challenges you to process your experiences deeply and to think hard about what's going on in your mind and emotions. As a result, you may find your ability to talk about playing and music begins to evolve to a higher and more thoughtful level. So, try to express yourself with clarity and precision. Go back and refine or elaborate your thoughts as ideas come to you.

Document, too, any questions that arise during the week: things to ask your music teacher, things to look up online. Perhaps you're wondering whether your brand of rosin or reed or valve oil or tuning slide grease is serving your purpose. Maybe you have a sudden curiosity about amplification that you want to follow up. Or you have questions about a composer or piece. Get it all down on paper here where it won't be lost.

As you're practicing, you'll undoubtedly have general fleeting thoughts about yourself and your playing. Some of those thoughts will be positive and encouraging. For example, you may feel great pride by your tone and tell yourself that you're making great progress. Record those positive thoughts. They'll help motivate and encourage you now and in the future. Writing them down will reinforce helpful ways of thinking about yourself and will enhance your self-esteem.

Of course, many musicians can also be plagued by self-criticism, or the demoralizingly negative thoughts that somehow seem to rise up automatically in our minds, do their damage, and remain in our background thoughts without ever being questioned or challenged. Rather than trying to suppress your self-critical thoughts, write them down in brief, too. Name the enemy. And then dispute those debilitating self-critical thoughts. Challenge them rationally.

One way to do that is to ask yourself what you would tell a best friend who had similar such thoughts. So, imagine if a friend happened to share your particular self-critical thought about practice, and said in great frustration, "I'm never never never going to be able to learn this passage!" How would you respond? Would you say, "You're right, have you thought about giving up entirely?" Of course not. You'd be the voice of reason. You'd suggest taking a break for a while, maybe breaking the passage into smaller chunks or playing more slowly, maybe suggesting more specific guidance from a teacher. But you would never validate the self-criticism.

Another way to defeat self-critical thoughts is to ask yourself if there's evidence a particular thought is true. You'll never learn that piece? Never is a mighty long time. There's something wrong with you? Perhaps it isn't "you," perhaps you just need another approach. You're a total failure as a musician if your song doesn't get online plays? Perhaps it's the platform, or its audience, or how it's promoted, or even something about the song itself. But nothing as pervasive as thinking yourself a total failure.

So, don't validate your own self-criticism. Challenge it. Dispute it. You may not be convinced the

Date: **March 15, 2021**

Listening / Watching / Reading Notes

Piece / Topic: **The Crazed Moon, Burt Flummox Trio**

The style and intensity of the piece were terrific. Loved the drumming, especially the fills, but also the drum groove in general. The piano was comping with repeating patterns, but still not predictable. And the way the piano played with dissonance.

Piece / Topic: **Walks Through Fog, OC Jazz Orchestra**

I liked the way the big band was arranged as if taking music on piano and giving separate notes to the horns. They spaced the sections well. Loved how the composer built the song in the intro, putting more and more until the whole song breaks out. Great that different instruments were featured.

Things to work on or be more mindful about

Remember to keep arms, wrists, hands, and fingers relaxed while playing fast lines.

Take a short break when playing starts getting imprecise.

Anticipate ascending and descending runs by moving the arm rather than the wrist.

Focus on dynamics and expression and not just speed for speed's sake.

Questions to answer

What chords does the phrygian dominant scale work best with?

How can I think of chord voicings more quickly?

Who are some musicians who have used the whole tone scale in compositions?

Positive thoughts and self-criticism

+ Started writing the piano and horn parts for an octet and felt really good about myself!

- Felt guilty and in a bad mood for having two short practices in a row.

Weekly Check-in

What most inspirerd you musically or creatively this week?

Hearing how Eric Dolphy helped Herbie Hancock explore new paths in melody, harmony, and rhythm.

Which assignment went best for you this week? Why?

Got the left hand down well enough on Donna Lee to start improvising better with my right hand.

What was the hardest part of your practicing this week?

Getting to a solid and confident enough point when playing songs in my repertoire.

What thought or idea do you want to keep in mind as you commence next week's practice?

Focus on dynamics and expression and not just speed for speed's sake.

Overall, how satisfied were you with your music practice this week? (1= not at all satisfied, 10 = very satisfied) ① ② ③ ④ ⑤ ⑥ ⑦✓ ⑧ ⑨ ⑩

first time. Or the second or third time. Especially when intense emotions get in the way. In calm and thoughtful moments, you will eventually find that you're able to come up with better and more compelling arguments against your self-critical thoughts.

The final section on the reflection page is a Weekly Check-in. Start with what excited you musically or creatively during the week. Perhaps it was another artist or a song that made you realize why you love music so much. Maybe you experienced something that you thought might be absolutely brilliant if captured in music. There might be a subtle emotion that you'd love to figure out how to work into your improvisation. These are the sort of things that keep you thinking and moving forward in your musical expression.

Next, write down which assignment went best for you during the week. It's important to acknowledge your musical victories. So, make an effort to perceive them. Document one so you can remind yourself that you can indeed move forward every time you pick up your instrument to practice. Practicing when and what you planned to practice is a victory. Going from mistake-ridden choppiness to mastery of one measure's turn is a victory. Extending your range by one whole step may be more of a victory than learning an entire new piece. Gather the positive evidence.

The musical victories that you acknowledge every week needn't be major accomplishments, like memorizing a long and complex concerto, booking a ten-city tour, or landing a six-figure recording contract. Musical growth results from a relentlessly continuing series of small and sometimes rather imperceptible victories.

Also, write down what was the hardest part of practicing during the week. It may be something specific to an assignment, such as getting a particular piece up to speed. Or it may be something general, such as finding the time to practice on busy days, or even motivating yourself to practice at all. Acknowledging challenges and difficulties is an important first step in being able to address or overcome them. It inspires many to keep the struggle in mind where potential solutions can be generated in the mental background. And it gives music teachers something on which they can bring to bear their knowledge and experience.

As with the weekly practice assignments, there is a place at the bottom of the page to check-in by assigning a weekly rating of your success. By rating your satisfaction with your week's practice, you can track over time how well you think your sessions have been going.

Progress Charts

As mentioned earlier, an important way of developing the habit of practice is to give yourself some tangible reward for your effort. Perhaps the most objective proof of your accomplishment is documented evidence of the time you spent practicing. When you see on paper the number of hours you spent practicing during your first week with AgendaMusica, you're likely to want to meet or exceed your practice time in subsequent weeks. Maintaining quantitative evidence of a practice streak can be tremendously rewarding and motivating. The number of hours of practice you've accumulated over a six-month period can be surprisingly and impressively high. Same with seeing that you've maintained a steady or increasing average practice-session length. You'd never know how much you've invested in your music unless you capture and chart your time.

Your subjective rating of your practice session quality can also be helpful in better understanding your musical growth, provided that your rating is thoughtful and honest. Maintaining a running record of your satisfaction with the quality of the week's practice can suggest when you might want or need to revisit your goals or weekly assignments.

Of course, there could be any number of other practice elements that you'd find value in measuring and charting. AgendaMusica provides space for you to customize graphic visualizations of any variables that are particularly relevant or important to you.

Repertoire

As one progresses through a lifetime of musical study, there's a tendency to learn a particular

Progress Charts

Total Weekly Practice Time

song or piece, practice it to perfection, perform it, and then put it into deep storage to devote time to the next newer or more challenging piece. Repeat the process with something new: learn, then store. Then on to another new piece. And another. An ever-moving conveyor belt moves one piece after another across the music stand. Consequently, the perfectly lovely music from last month or last year languishes and fades from memory.

Of course, sometimes when we don't know what to play during a practice session, a piece from the past squeamishly raises its hand and struggles to the fingers. The first few measures might come out alright, but after that, well, things start to get unsteady. That's the way our memories work. Learning fades without practice.

As a musician, it's important to nurture and maintain your repertoire. Remember that a repertoire is defined not just as pieces that you've learned, or pieces that you have some vague familiarity with. Remember that a repertoire consists of the pieces that one is prepared to perform

Repertoire

Title — Plus sign for week added to repertoire; circle or check weeks on which included in Weekly Practice Journal

Title	Added
Nocturne from second concerto	+ (week 1)
Le Cygne Sauvage	+ (week 6)
Waltz (Eierkuchen)	+ (week 10)
Meditation in C#	+ (week 16)
Theme from Mabinogion	+ (week 19)

What single musical accomplishment made you the proudest?
Won the "Outstanding Soloist" award in a competition among jazz bands from 8 other high schools
by playing a solo on Nat Adderley's Work Song. Got a trophy that proudly sits on our piano.

What other musical accomplishments also made you very proud?
Composed and arranged a piece for my 14-musician Saturday ensemble at Center for Performing
Arts that was actually played in front of an audience at the year end show. Transcribed Urbie
Green's solo on Triste and learned to play it at the same high register as him.

What personal insights and observations arose during your past six months of practice?
I sometimes feel too tired to practice especially after a long day at school, so I want to avoid it
and play video games, but when I don't practice I always end up regretting that I didn't and feel
bad for lying to myself because I'm never really THAT tired to pick up my trombone.

without difficulty. It's not just learning things; it's learning things well enough to be able to perform at the drop of a hat.

The Repertoire page, which for the sake of convenience appears at the very end of AgendaMusica, helps you remember the names of the pieces you've learned, when you learned them, and the weeks in which you've included each in the Repertoire section of your Weekly Practice Journal. Even just a brief few minutes of practice each session can help keep the pieces you've worked so hard on fresh enough to be able to play on request.

Notes pages

On the pages that follow the Weekly Practice Journal pages, you'll find pages for three different types of notes: Tips and Exercise Notes, Listening Notes, and Thoughts and Meditations.

The pages of Practice Tips and Exercise Notes give you space in which to write down ideas, techniques, and practice exercises that aren't better documented in your notebook of music manuscript paper. Let's say you watch an online video that describes a certain way of thinking about intonation. Or your music teacher gives you a big and memorable way to conceptualize improvisation. Or a fellow musician shares an exercise that's led to great improvement in finger speed.

Here's a place where you can give each a title, detailed description, and identify the source.

The pages of Listening Notes with expanded space give you an additional place where you can record your impressions of particular musical pieces you've heard or watched, or music-related articles or books that you've read. Once you've taken the time and effort to commit your reactions or evaluations to paper, they become a permanent part of your musical development. You'll have created a reference of your mental processes and analyses that will show you what you thought and when you thought it.

There are pages, too, for Thoughts and Meditations. Use these pages to journal what you're thinking about your musical life in general. What do you want to document and remember? Why you like or don't like a particular genre of music? What it means to think of yourself as a musician? What you mentally told yourself and how you responded emotionally after a good or bad performance? Hopes. Dreams. Anything. Get it all down on paper so you can someday look back fondly on those special moments in time.

6-month Reflection and The Path Forward

Finally, at the end of six months, it's a reasonable time in which to take stock of how you've been practicing and to contemplate the bigger picture.

What would happen if you didn't change a thing about how you practice?
I would probably get better at playing, but I might not get as far in my playing as my friends in the jazz band, and that would make me feel bad because I know I'm competitive, but also because I'd feel that by not doing my best was somehow letting them down.

How would you like for practice to be different?
I would like to find a way to get so into my practice that I lose track of time. I don't want practice to ever feel like a chore that I have to get done as quickly as possible. I love playing, but sometimes I just watch the clock. I don't like feeling that way.

What would you be willing to try?
My teacher told me that I should slow myself down. Rather than playing through the whole song just to finish it, I should focus on getting one or two measures down perfectly and being satisfied that doing that was an accomplishment. He calls it "deep practice" and I want to do it more.

On these reflection pages are 18 questions to encourage you to think deeply about your recent months of practice and to think forwardly about where you'd like your practice to go from here.

Start with what worked well and any particularly salient insights that revealed themselves. Identify where the energy came from to practice as hard as you did. Think about who or what inspired you to keep going during the inevitable times when practicing was challenging or difficult. Or what feelings or events pushed you to learn a new piece, write a specific composition, or practice in a certain style or with a distinct dynamic.

Think, too, about what worked less well. The obstacles you faced. Some of those hindrances may have come about from external factors, such as other school, work, or family duties, demands, and responsibilities. Other practicing impediments may have been due to internal factors, such as the negative and self-critical thoughts you have about yourself, your musical ability, your prospects as a musician.

Writing obstacles down allows you to get them out in the open and available for reflection. Otherwise your thoughts flutter randomly and chaotically in your mind. Pin your thoughts to the page. You can then brainstorm ideas and negotiate solutions for the practical or logistical barriers. And you can work on your own or with a coach to examine and challenge any negative and unhelpful thoughts that might be holding back more progress.

Everything you do musically and otherwise is connected to the larger world outside of yourself. As you reflect on your practicing over the past six months, think about what you've been most grateful for in the grander context of life and the universe. Contemplate what most made you feel part of the wonder and joy of being alive. Then express your gratitude on paper to help you document and remember your vital relationship to the cosmos. Doing so can intensify your appreciation of the good times and re-center you when the times are difficult. Find a word, phrase, or thought that affirms your existence and your place in the world to build lasting connection, optimism, and hopefulness.

Goal setting

Identify 3 to 5 most meaningful goals, then what you'll need to do to achieve each. (Ask your teacher or refer to the list, below.)

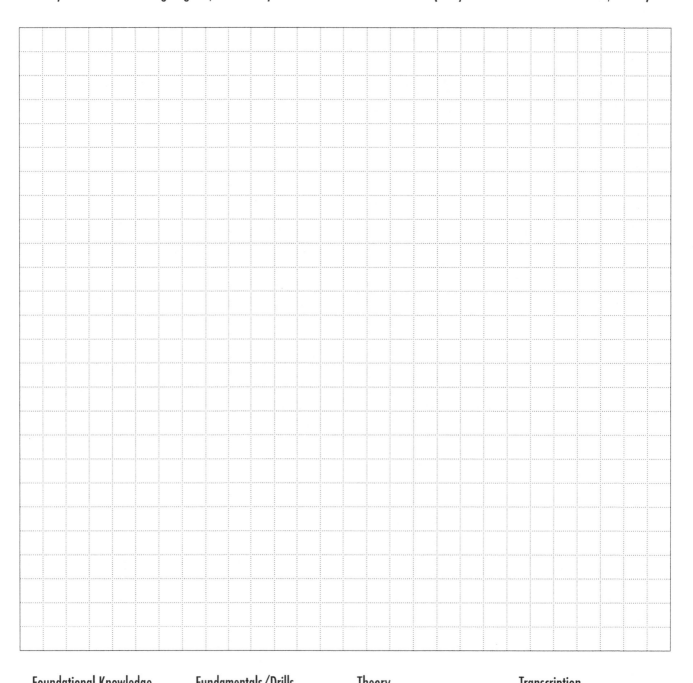

Foundational Knowledge	Fundamentals/Drills	Theory	Transcription
Musical staff	Sight-reading	Scales and modes	Rhytmic notation
Time signatures	Breathing/posture	Chords	Pitch notation
Note/rest values	Embouchure/bowing	Arpeggios	Solfege
Rhythmic notation	Finger dexterity/speed	Melody	Time signature
Pitch notation	Finger strength	Harmony	Chord identification
Key signatures	Range-building	Counterpoint	Song structure

Make sure your goals are "SMART": Specific, Measurable, Attainable, Relevant, and Time-bound (think 6 months to 1 year).

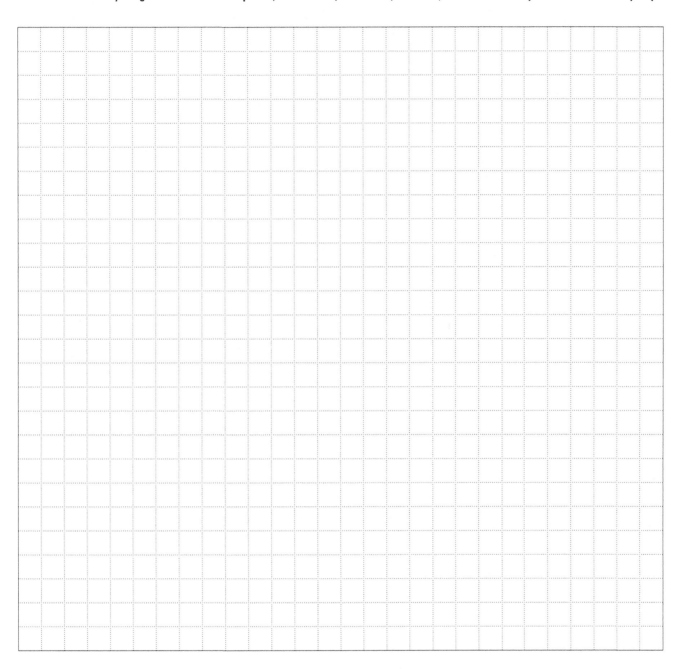

Composition	Improvisation	Repertoire	Performance
Listening and analysis	Listen to others	Listening	Self-talk
Emulation	Transcribe others	Identifying new pieces	Visualization
Form/structure study	Analyze transcriptions	Learning new pieces	Stage presence development
Idea generation	Practice transcriptions	Recording learned pieces	Program development
Idea development	Improvise against	Critiquing performance	Record rehearsals
Manuscript	chord progressions		Critical review

Goal setting

Identify 3 to 5 most meaningful goals, then what you'll need to do to achieve each. (Ask your teacher or refer to the list, below.)

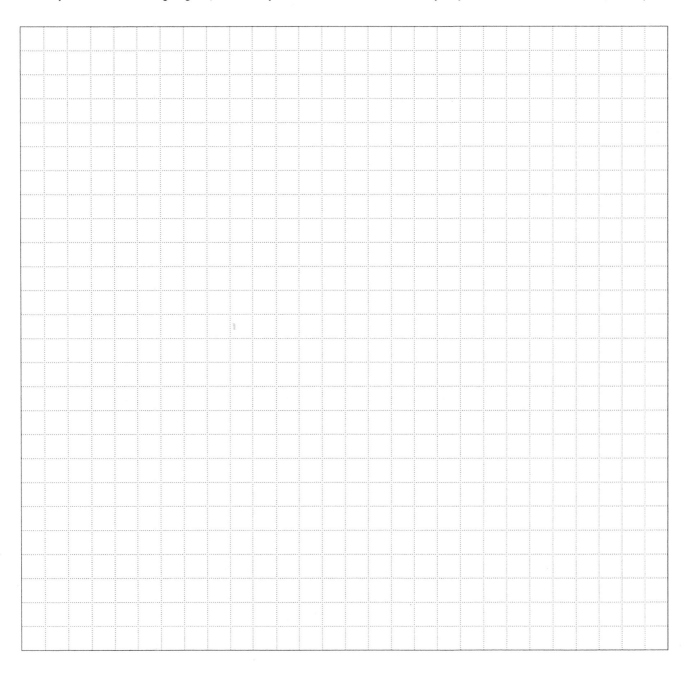

Foundational Knowledge	Fundamentals/Drills	Theory	Transcription
Musical staff	Sight-reading	Scales and modes	Rhytmic notation
Time signatures	Breathing/posture	Chords	Pitch notation
Note/rest values	Embouchure/bowing	Arpeggios	Solfege
Rhythmic notation	Finger dexterity/speed	Melody	Time signature
Pitch notation	Finger strength	Harmony	Chord identification
Key signatures	Range-building	Counterpoint	Song structure

Make sure your goals are "SMART": Specific, Measurable, Attainable, Relevant, and Time-bound (think 6 months to 1 year).

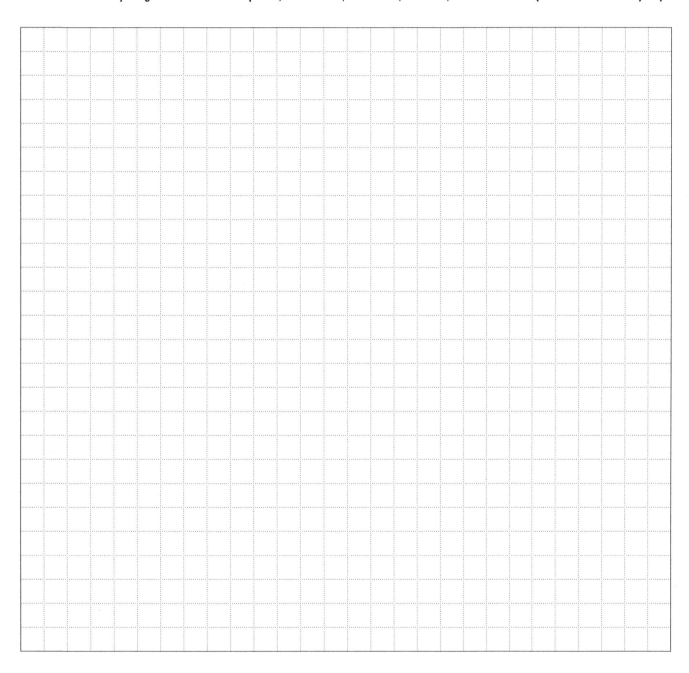

Composition

Listening and analysis
Emulation
Form/structure study
Idea generation
Idea development
Manuscript

Improvisation

Listen to others
Transcribe others
Analyze transcriptions
Practice transcriptions
Improvise against
    chord progressions

Repertoire

Listening
Identifying new pieces
Learning new pieces
Recording learned pieces
Critiquing performance

Performance

Self-talk
Visualization
Stage presence development
Program development
Record rehearsals
Critical review

Week 1: Reflection

Date:

Listening / Watching / Reading Notes

Piece / Topic: | Piece / Topic:

Things to work on or be more mindful about

Questions to answer

Positive thoughts and self-criticism

Weekly Check-in

What most inspired you musically or creatively this week?

Which assignment went best for you this week? Why?

What was the hardest part of your practicing this week?

What thought or idea do you want to keep in mind as you commence next week's practice?

Overall, how satisfied were you with your music practice this week? (1= not at all satisfied, 10 = very satisfied) ① ② ③ ④ ⑤ ⑥ ⑦ ⑧ ⑨ ⑩

Date: Day of the week

Warm-up / Preparation

	reps/mins	○	○	○	○	○	○	○
	reps/mins	○	○	○	○	○	○	○
	reps/mins	○	○	○	○	○	○	○
	reps/mins	○	○	○	○	○	○	○
	reps/mins	○	○	○	○	○	○	○

Exploration / Improvisation / Discovery

	mins	○	○	○	○	○	○	○
	mins	○	○	○	○	○	○	○
	mins	○	○	○	○	○	○	○

Fundamentals / Drills

	reps/mins	○	○	○	○	○	○	○
	reps/mins	○	○	○	○	○	○	○
	reps/mins	○	○	○	○	○	○	○
	reps/mins	○	○	○	○	○	○	○
	reps/mins	○	○	○	○	○	○	○
	reps/mins	○	○	○	○	○	○	○
	reps/mins	○	○	○	○	○	○	○

Week's Focus

	reps/mins	○	○	○	○	○	○	○
	reps/mins	○	○	○	○	○	○	○
	reps/mins	○	○	○	○	○	○	○
	reps/mins	○	○	○	○	○	○	○
	reps/mins	○	○	○	○	○	○	○
	reps/mins	○	○	○	○	○	○	○
	reps/mins	○	○	○	○	○	○	○

Repertoire / Review / Rehearsal

	reps/mins	○	○	○	○	○	○	○
	reps/mins	○	○	○	○	○	○	○
	reps/mins	○	○	○	○	○	○	○
	reps/mins	○	○	○	○	○	○	○
	reps/mins	○	○	○	○	○	○	○

Daily Summary

Practice session quality (rate ☺,☺,☹)								
Length of day's practice session (mins)								
Summary of week's practice time (mins)	Total / Days = Average							

Week 2: Reflection

Date:

Listening / Watching / Reading Notes

Piece / Topic:

Piece / Topic:

Things to work on or be more mindful about

Questions to answer

Positive thoughts and self-criticism

Weekly Check-in

What most inspired you musically or creatively this week?

Which assignment went best for you this week? Why?

What was the hardest part of your practicing this week?

What thought or idea do you want to keep in mind as you commence next week's practice?

Overall, how satisfied were you with your music practice this week? (1= not at all satisfied, 10 = very satisfied)   ① ② ③ ④ ⑤ ⑥ ⑦ ⑧ ⑨ ⑩

Date: Day of the week

Warm-up / Preparation

	reps/mins
	reps/mins
	reps/mins
	reps/mins
	reps/mins

Exploration / Improvisation / Discovery

	mins
	mins
	mins

Fundamentals / Drills

	reps/mins
	reps/mins
	reps/mins
	reps/mins
	reps/mins
	reps/mins
	reps/mins

Week's Focus

	reps/mins
	reps/mins
	reps/mins
	reps/mins
	reps/mins
	reps/mins
	reps/mins

Repertoire / Review / Rehearsal

	reps/mins
	reps/mins
	reps/mins
	reps/mins
	reps/mins

Daily Summary

Practice session quality (rate ☺,☺,☺)	
Length of day's practice session (mins)	
Summary of week's practice time (mins)	Total / Days = Average

Week 3: Reflection

Date:

Listening / Watching / Reading Notes

Piece / Topic:

Piece / Topic:

Things to work on or be more mindful about

Questions to answer

Positive thoughts and self-criticism

Weekly Check-in

What most inspired you musically or creatively this week?

Which assignment went best for you this week? Why?

What was the hardest part of your practicing this week?

What thought or idea do you want to keep in mind as you commence next week's practice?

Overall, how satisfied were you with your music practice this week? (1= not at all satisfied, 10 = very satisfied) ① ② ③ ④ ⑤ ⑥ ⑦ ⑧ ⑨ ⑩

Date: Day of the week

Warm-up / Preparation

_____ reps/mins	○	○	○	○	○	○	○
_____ reps/mins	○	○	○	○	○	○	○
_____ reps/mins	○	○	○	○	○	○	○
_____ reps/mins	○	○	○	○	○	○	○
_____ reps/mins	○	○	○	○	○	○	○

Exploration / Improvisation / Discovery

_____ mins	○	○	○	○	○	○	○
_____ mins	○	○	○	○	○	○	○
_____ mins	○	○	○	○	○	○	○

Fundamentals / Drills

_____ reps/mins	○	○	○	○	○	○	○
_____ reps/mins	○	○	○	○	○	○	○
_____ reps/mins	○	○	○	○	○	○	○
_____ reps/mins	○	○	○	○	○	○	○
_____ reps/mins	○	○	○	○	○	○	○
_____ reps/mins	○	○	○	○	○	○	○
_____ reps/mins	○	○	○	○	○	○	○

Week's Focus

_____ reps/mins	○	○	○	○	○	○	○
_____ reps/mins	○	○	○	○	○	○	○
_____ reps/mins	○	○	○	○	○	○	○
_____ reps/mins	○	○	○	○	○	○	○
_____ reps/mins	○	○	○	○	○	○	○
_____ reps/mins	○	○	○	○	○	○	○
_____ reps/mins	○	○	○	○	○	○	○

Repertoire / Review / Rehearsal

_____ reps/mins	○	○	○	○	○	○	○
_____ reps/mins	○	○	○	○	○	○	○
_____ reps/mins	○	○	○	○	○	○	○
_____ reps/mins	○	○	○	○	○	○	○
_____ reps/mins	○	○	○	○	○	○	○

Daily Summary

Practice session quality (rate ☺,☺,☹)							
Length of day's practice session (mins)							
Summary of week's practice time (mins)	Total /	Days =		Average			

Week 4: Reflection

Date:

Listening / Watching / Reading Notes

Piece / Topic:

Piece / Topic:

Things to work on or be more mindful about

Questions to answer

Positive thoughts and self-criticism

Weekly Check-in

What most inspired you musically or creatively this week?

Which assignment went best for you this week? Why?

What was the hardest part of your practicing this week?

What thought or idea do you want to keep in mind as you commence next week's practice?

Overall, how satisfied were you with your music practice this week? (1= not at all satisfied, 10 = very satisfied)   ① ② ③ ④ ⑤ ⑥ ⑦ ⑧ ⑨ ⑩

Date: _____   Day of the week

Warm-up / Preparation

_____ reps/mins	○	○	○	○	○	○	○
_____ reps/mins	○	○	○	○	○	○	○
_____ reps/mins	○	○	○	○	○	○	○
_____ reps/mins	○	○	○	○	○	○	○
_____ reps/mins	○	○	○	○	○	○	○

Exploration / Improvisation / Discovery

_____ mins	○	○	○	○	○	○	○
_____ mins	○	○	○	○	○	○	○
_____ mins	○	○	○	○	○	○	○

Fundamentals / Drills

_____ reps/mins	○	○	○	○	○	○	○
_____ reps/mins	○	○	○	○	○	○	○
_____ reps/mins	○	○	○	○	○	○	○
_____ reps/mins	○	○	○	○	○	○	○
_____ reps/mins	○	○	○	○	○	○	○
_____ reps/mins	○	○	○	○	○	○	○
_____ reps/mins	○	○	○	○	○	○	○

Week's Focus

_____ reps/mins	○	○	○	○	○	○	○
_____ reps/mins	○	○	○	○	○	○	○
_____ reps/mins	○	○	○	○	○	○	○
_____ reps/mins	○	○	○	○	○	○	○
_____ reps/mins	○	○	○	○	○	○	○
_____ reps/mins	○	○	○	○	○	○	○
_____ reps/mins	○	○	○	○	○	○	○

Repertoire / Review / Rehearsal

_____ reps/mins	○	○	○	○	○	○	○
_____ reps/mins	○	○	○	○	○	○	○
_____ reps/mins	○	○	○	○	○	○	○
_____ reps/mins	○	○	○	○	○	○	○
_____ reps/mins	○	○	○	○	○	○	○

Daily Summary

Practice session quality (rate ☺,☺,☹)							
Length of day's practice session (mins)							
Summary of week's practice time (mins)	Total / Days = Average						

Week 5: Reflection

Date:

Listening / Watching / Reading Notes

Piece / Topic:

Piece / Topic:

Things to work on or be more mindful about

Questions to answer

Positive thoughts and self-criticism

Weekly Check-in

What most inspired you musically or creatively this week?

Which assignment went best for you this week? Why?

What was the hardest part of your practicing this week?

What thought or idea do you want to keep in mind as you commence next week's practice?

Overall, how satisfied were you with your music practice this week? (1= not at all satisfied, 10 = very satisfied) ① ② ③ ④ ⑤ ⑥ ⑦ ⑧ ⑨ ⑩

Date: Day of the week

Warm-up / Preparation

reps/mins	○ ○ ○ ○ ○ ○ ○
reps/mins	○ ○ ○ ○ ○ ○ ○
reps/mins	○ ○ ○ ○ ○ ○ ○
reps/mins	○ ○ ○ ○ ○ ○ ○
reps/mins	○ ○ ○ ○ ○ ○ ○

Exploration / Improvisation / Discovery

mins	○ ○ ○ ○ ○ ○ ○
mins	○ ○ ○ ○ ○ ○ ○
mins	○ ○ ○ ○ ○ ○ ○

Fundamentals / Drills

reps/mins	○ ○ ○ ○ ○ ○ ○
reps/mins	○ ○ ○ ○ ○ ○ ○
reps/mins	○ ○ ○ ○ ○ ○ ○
reps/mins	○ ○ ○ ○ ○ ○ ○
reps/mins	○ ○ ○ ○ ○ ○ ○
reps/mins	○ ○ ○ ○ ○ ○ ○
reps/mins	○ ○ ○ ○ ○ ○ ○

Week's Focus

reps/mins	○ ○ ○ ○ ○ ○ ○
reps/mins	○ ○ ○ ○ ○ ○ ○
reps/mins	○ ○ ○ ○ ○ ○ ○
reps/mins	○ ○ ○ ○ ○ ○ ○
reps/mins	○ ○ ○ ○ ○ ○ ○
reps/mins	○ ○ ○ ○ ○ ○ ○
reps/mins	○ ○ ○ ○ ○ ○ ○

Repertoire / Review / Rehearsal

reps/mins	○ ○ ○ ○ ○ ○ ○
reps/mins	○ ○ ○ ○ ○ ○ ○
reps/mins	○ ○ ○ ○ ○ ○ ○
reps/mins	○ ○ ○ ○ ○ ○ ○
reps/mins	○ ○ ○ ○ ○ ○ ○

Daily Summary

Practice session quality (rate ☺,☺,☹)	
Length of day's practice session (mins)	
Summary of week's practice time (mins)	Total / Days = Average

Week 6: Reflection

Date:

Listening / Watching / Reading Notes

Piece / Topic:	Piece / Topic:

Things to work on or be more mindful about

Questions to answer

Positive thoughts and self-criticism

Weekly Check-in

What most inspired you musically or creatively this week?

Which assignment went best for you this week? Why?

What was the hardest part of your practicing this week?

What thought or idea do you want to keep in mind as you commence next week's practice?

Overall, how satisfied were you with your music practice this week? (1= not at all satisfied, 10 = very satisfied) ① ② ③ ④ ⑤ ⑥ ⑦ ⑧ ⑨ ⑩

Date: _____

	Day of the week							

Warm-up / Preparation

_____ reps/mins	○	○	○	○	○	○	○
_____ reps/mins	○	○	○	○	○	○	○
_____ reps/mins	○	○	○	○	○	○	○
_____ reps/mins	○	○	○	○	○	○	○
_____ reps/mins	○	○	○	○	○	○	○

Exploration / Improvisation / Discovery

_____ mins	○	○	○	○	○	○	○
_____ mins	○	○	○	○	○	○	○
_____ mins	○	○	○	○	○	○	○

Fundamentals / Drills

_____ reps/mins	○	○	○	○	○	○	○
_____ reps/mins	○	○	○	○	○	○	○
_____ reps/mins	○	○	○	○	○	○	○
_____ reps/mins	○	○	○	○	○	○	○
_____ reps/mins	○	○	○	○	○	○	○
_____ reps/mins	○	○	○	○	○	○	○
_____ reps/mins	○	○	○	○	○	○	○

Week's Focus

_____ reps/mins	○	○	○	○	○	○	○
_____ reps/mins	○	○	○	○	○	○	○
_____ reps/mins	○	○	○	○	○	○	○
_____ reps/mins	○	○	○	○	○	○	○
_____ reps/mins	○	○	○	○	○	○	○
_____ reps/mins	○	○	○	○	○	○	○
_____ reps/mins	○	○	○	○	○	○	○

Repertoire / Review / Rehearsal

_____ reps/mins	○	○	○	○	○	○	○
_____ reps/mins	○	○	○	○	○	○	○
_____ reps/mins	○	○	○	○	○	○	○
_____ reps/mins	○	○	○	○	○	○	○
_____ reps/mins	○	○	○	○	○	○	○

Daily Summary

Practice session quality (rate ☺,☺,☹)							
Length of day's practice session (mins)							
Summary of week's practice time (mins)	Total ___ / Days ___ = Average ___						

Week 7: Reflection

Date:

Listening / Watching / Reading Notes

Piece / Topic:

Piece / Topic:

Things to work on or be more mindful about

Questions to answer

Positive thoughts and self-criticism

Weekly Check-in

What most inspired you musically or creatively this week?

Which assignment went best for you this week? Why?

What was the hardest part of your practicing this week?

What thought or idea do you want to keep in mind as you commence next week's practice?

Overall, how satisfied were you with your music practice this week? (1= not at all satisfied, 10 = very satisfied) ① ② ③ ④ ⑤ ⑥ ⑦ ⑧ ⑨ ⑩

Date: _____   Day of the week

Warm-up / Preparation

_____	_____ reps/mins	○	○	○	○	○	○	○
_____	_____ reps/mins	○	○	○	○	○	○	○
_____	_____ reps/mins	○	○	○	○	○	○	○
_____	_____ reps/mins	○	○	○	○	○	○	○
_____	_____ reps/mins	○	○	○	○	○	○	○

Exploration / Improvisation / Discovery

_____	_____ mins	○	○	○	○	○	○	○
_____	_____ mins	○	○	○	○	○	○	○
_____	_____ mins	○	○	○	○	○	○	○

Fundamentals / Drills

_____	_____ reps/mins	○	○	○	○	○	○	○
_____	_____ reps/mins	○	○	○	○	○	○	○
_____	_____ reps/mins	○	○	○	○	○	○	○
_____	_____ reps/mins	○	○	○	○	○	○	○
_____	_____ reps/mins	○	○	○	○	○	○	○
_____	_____ reps/mins	○	○	○	○	○	○	○
_____	_____ reps/mins	○	○	○	○	○	○	○

Week's Focus

_____	_____ reps/mins	○	○	○	○	○	○	○
_____	_____ reps/mins	○	○	○	○	○	○	○
_____	_____ reps/mins	○	○	○	○	○	○	○
_____	_____ reps/mins	○	○	○	○	○	○	○
_____	_____ reps/mins	○	○	○	○	○	○	○
_____	_____ reps/mins	○	○	○	○	○	○	○
_____	_____ reps/mins	○	○	○	○	○	○	○

Repertoire / Review / Rehearsal

_____	_____ reps/mins	○	○	○	○	○	○	○
_____	_____ reps/mins	○	○	○	○	○	○	○
_____	_____ reps/mins	○	○	○	○	○	○	○
_____	_____ reps/mins	○	○	○	○	○	○	○
_____	_____ reps/mins	○	○	○	○	○	○	○

Daily Summary

Practice session quality (rate ☺,☺,☹)								
Length of day's practice session (mins)								
Summary of week's practice time (mins)	Total /		Days =			Average		

Week 8: Reflection

Date:

Listening / Watching / Reading Notes

Piece / Topic:	Piece / Topic:

Things to work on or be more mindful about

Questions to answer

Positive thoughts and self-criticism

Weekly Check-in

What most inspired you musically or creatively this week?

Which assignment went best for you this week? Why?

What was the hardest part of your practicing this week?

What thought or idea do you want to keep in mind as you commence next week's practice?

Overall, how satisfied were you with your music practice this week? (1= not at all satisfied, 10 = very satisfied) ① ② ③ ④ ⑤ ⑥ ⑦ ⑧ ⑨ ⑩

Date: Day of the week

Warm-up / Preparation

	reps/mins	○	○	○	○	○	○	○
	reps/mins	○	○	○	○	○	○	○
	reps/mins	○	○	○	○	○	○	○
	reps/mins	○	○	○	○	○	○	○
	reps/mins	○	○	○	○	○	○	○

Exploration / Improvisation / Discovery

	mins	○	○	○	○	○	○	○
	mins	○	○	○	○	○	○	○
	mins	○	○	○	○	○	○	○

Fundamentals / Drills

	reps/mins	○	○	○	○	○	○	○
	reps/mins	○	○	○	○	○	○	○
	reps/mins	○	○	○	○	○	○	○
	reps/mins	○	○	○	○	○	○	○
	reps/mins	○	○	○	○	○	○	○
	reps/mins	○	○	○	○	○	○	○
	reps/mins	○	○	○	○	○	○	○

Week's Focus

	reps/mins	○	○	○	○	○	○	○
	reps/mins	○	○	○	○	○	○	○
	reps/mins	○	○	○	○	○	○	○
	reps/mins	○	○	○	○	○	○	○
	reps/mins	○	○	○	○	○	○	○
	reps/mins	○	○	○	○	○	○	○
	reps/mins	○	○	○	○	○	○	○

Repertoire / Review / Rehearsal

	reps/mins	○	○	○	○	○	○	○
	reps/mins	○	○	○	○	○	○	○
	reps/mins	○	○	○	○	○	○	○
	reps/mins	○	○	○	○	○	○	○
	reps/mins	○	○	○	○	○	○	○

Daily Summary

Practice session quality (rate ☺,☻,☹)	
Length of day's practice session (mins)	
Summary of week's practice time (mins)	Total / Days = Average

Week 9: Reflection

Date:

Listening / Watching / Reading Notes

Piece / Topic:

Piece / Topic:

Things to work on or be more mindful about

Questions to answer

Positive thoughts and self-criticism

Weekly Check-in

What most inspired you musically or creatively this week?

Which assignment went best for you this week? Why?

What was the hardest part of your practicing this week?

What thought or idea do you want to keep in mind as you commence next week's practice?

| Overall, how satisfied were you with your music practice this week? (1= not at all satisfied, 10 = very satisfied) | ① | ② | ③ | ④ | ⑤ | ⑥ | ⑦ | ⑧ | ⑨ | ⑩ |

Date: Day of the week

Warm-up / Preparation

_____ reps/mins	○	○	○	○	○	○	○
_____ reps/mins	○	○	○	○	○	○	○
_____ reps/mins	○	○	○	○	○	○	○
_____ reps/mins	○	○	○	○	○	○	○
_____ reps/mins	○	○	○	○	○	○	○

Exploration / Improvisation / Discovery

_____ mins	○	○	○	○	○	○	○
_____ mins	○	○	○	○	○	○	○
_____ mins	○	○	○	○	○	○	○

Fundamentals / Drills

_____ reps/mins	○	○	○	○	○	○	○
_____ reps/mins	○	○	○	○	○	○	○
_____ reps/mins	○	○	○	○	○	○	○
_____ reps/mins	○	○	○	○	○	○	○
_____ reps/mins	○	○	○	○	○	○	○
_____ reps/mins	○	○	○	○	○	○	○
_____ reps/mins	○	○	○	○	○	○	○

Week's Focus

_____ reps/mins	○	○	○	○	○	○	○
_____ reps/mins	○	○	○	○	○	○	○
_____ reps/mins	○	○	○	○	○	○	○
_____ reps/mins	○	○	○	○	○	○	○
_____ reps/mins	○	○	○	○	○	○	○
_____ reps/mins	○	○	○	○	○	○	○
_____ reps/mins	○	○	○	○	○	○	○

Repertoire / Review / Rehearsal

_____ reps/mins	○	○	○	○	○	○	○
_____ reps/mins	○	○	○	○	○	○	○
_____ reps/mins	○	○	○	○	○	○	○
_____ reps/mins	○	○	○	○	○	○	○
_____ reps/mins	○	○	○	○	○	○	○

Daily Summary

Practice session quality (rate ☺,☺,☹)							
Length of day's practice session (mins)							
Summary of week's practice time (mins)	Total / Days = Average						

Week 10: Reflection

Date:

Listening / Watching / Reading Notes

Piece / Topic:	Piece / Topic:

Things to work on or be more mindful about

Questions to answer

Positive thoughts and self-criticism

Weekly Check-in

What most inspired you musically or creatively this week?

Which assignment went best for you this week? Why?

What was the hardest part of your practicing this week?

What thought or idea do you want to keep in mind as you commence next week's practice?

| Overall, how satisfied were you with your music practice this week? (1= not at all satisfied, 10 = very satisfied) | ① | ② | ③ | ④ | ⑤ | ⑥ | ⑦ | ⑧ | ⑨ | ⑩ |

Date: Day of the week

Warm-up / Preparation

	reps/mins	○	○	○	○	○	○	○
	reps/mins	○	○	○	○	○	○	○
	reps/mins	○	○	○	○	○	○	○
	reps/mins	○	○	○	○	○	○	○
	reps/mins	○	○	○	○	○	○	○

Exploration / Improvisation / Discovery

	mins	○	○	○	○	○	○	○
	mins	○	○	○	○	○	○	○
	mins	○	○	○	○	○	○	○

Fundamentals / Drills

	reps/mins	○	○	○	○	○	○	○
	reps/mins	○	○	○	○	○	○	○
	reps/mins	○	○	○	○	○	○	○
	reps/mins	○	○	○	○	○	○	○
	reps/mins	○	○	○	○	○	○	○
	reps/mins	○	○	○	○	○	○	○
	reps/mins	○	○	○	○	○	○	○

Week's Focus

	reps/mins	○	○	○	○	○	○	○
	reps/mins	○	○	○	○	○	○	○
	reps/mins	○	○	○	○	○	○	○
	reps/mins	○	○	○	○	○	○	○
	reps/mins	○	○	○	○	○	○	○
	reps/mins	○	○	○	○	○	○	○
	reps/mins	○	○	○	○	○	○	○

Repertoire / Review / Rehearsal

	reps/mins	○	○	○	○	○	○	○
	reps/mins	○	○	○	○	○	○	○
	reps/mins	○	○	○	○	○	○	○
	reps/mins	○	○	○	○	○	○	○
	reps/mins	○	○	○	○	○	○	○

Daily Summary

Practice session quality (rate ☺,☺,☹)	
Length of day's practice session (mins)	
Summary of week's practice time (mins)	Total / Days = Average

Week 11: Reflection

Date:

Listening / Watching / Reading Notes

Piece / Topic:	Piece / Topic:

Things to work on or be more mindful about

Questions to answer

Positive thoughts and self-criticism

Weekly Check-in

What most inspired you musically or creatively this week?

Which assignment went best for you this week? Why?

What was the hardest part of your practicing this week?

What thought or idea do you want to keep in mind as you commence next week's practice?

Overall, how satisfied were you with your music practice this week? (1= not at all satisfied, 10 = very satisfied) ① ② ③ ④ ⑤ ⑥ ⑦ ⑧ ⑨ ⑩

Date: _____

Day of the week

Warm-up / Preparation

	reps/mins	○	○	○	○	○	○	○
	reps/mins	○	○	○	○	○	○	○
	reps/mins	○	○	○	○	○	○	○
	reps/mins	○	○	○	○	○	○	○
	reps/mins	○	○	○	○	○	○	○

Exploration / Improvisation / Discovery

	mins	○	○	○	○	○	○	○
	mins	○	○	○	○	○	○	○
	mins	○	○	○	○	○	○	○

Fundamentals / Drills

	reps/mins	○	○	○	○	○	○	○
	reps/mins	○	○	○	○	○	○	○
	reps/mins	○	○	○	○	○	○	○
	reps/mins	○	○	○	○	○	○	○
	reps/mins	○	○	○	○	○	○	○
	reps/mins	○	○	○	○	○	○	○
	reps/mins	○	○	○	○	○	○	○

Week's Focus

	reps/mins	○	○	○	○	○	○	○
	reps/mins	○	○	○	○	○	○	○
	reps/mins	○	○	○	○	○	○	○
	reps/mins	○	○	○	○	○	○	○
	reps/mins	○	○	○	○	○	○	○
	reps/mins	○	○	○	○	○	○	○
	reps/mins	○	○	○	○	○	○	○

Repertoire / Review / Rehearsal

	reps/mins	○	○	○	○	○	○	○
	reps/mins	○	○	○	○	○	○	○
	reps/mins	○	○	○	○	○	○	○
	reps/mins	○	○	○	○	○	○	○
	reps/mins	○	○	○	○	○	○	○

Daily Summary

Practice session quality (rate ☺,☺,☹)							
Length of day's practice session (mins)							
Summary of week's practice time (mins)	Total / Days = Average

Week 12: Reflection

Date:

Listening / Watching / Reading Notes

Piece / Topic:

Piece / Topic:

Things to work on or be more mindful about

Questions to answer

Positive thoughts and self-criticism

Weekly Check-in

What most inspired you musically or creatively this week?

Which assignment went best for you this week? Why?

What was the hardest part of your practicing this week?

What thought or idea do you want to keep in mind as you commence next week's practice?

| Overall, how satisfied were you with your music practice this week? (1= not at all satisfied, 10 = very satisfied) | ① | ② | ③ | ④ | ⑤ | ⑥ | ⑦ | ⑧ | ⑨ | ⑩ |

Date: Day of the week

Warm-up / Preparation

_____ reps/mins	○	○	○	○	○	○	○
_____ reps/mins	○	○	○	○	○	○	○
_____ reps/mins	○	○	○	○	○	○	○
_____ reps/mins	○	○	○	○	○	○	○
_____ reps/mins	○	○	○	○	○	○	○

Exploration / Improvisation / Discovery

_____ mins	○	○	○	○	○	○	○
_____ mins	○	○	○	○	○	○	○
_____ mins	○	○	○	○	○	○	○

Fundamentals / Drills

_____ reps/mins	○	○	○	○	○	○	○
_____ reps/mins	○	○	○	○	○	○	○
_____ reps/mins	○	○	○	○	○	○	○
_____ reps/mins	○	○	○	○	○	○	○
_____ reps/mins	○	○	○	○	○	○	○
_____ reps/mins	○	○	○	○	○	○	○
_____ reps/mins	○	○	○	○	○	○	○

Week's Focus

_____ reps/mins	○	○	○	○	○	○	○
_____ reps/mins	○	○	○	○	○	○	○
_____ reps/mins	○	○	○	○	○	○	○
_____ reps/mins	○	○	○	○	○	○	○
_____ reps/mins	○	○	○	○	○	○	○
_____ reps/mins	○	○	○	○	○	○	○
_____ reps/mins	○	○	○	○	○	○	○

Repertoire / Review / Rehearsal

_____ reps/mins	○	○	○	○	○	○	○
_____ reps/mins	○	○	○	○	○	○	○
_____ reps/mins	○	○	○	○	○	○	○
_____ reps/mins	○	○	○	○	○	○	○
_____ reps/mins	○	○	○	○	○	○	○

Daily Summary

Practice session quality (rate ☺,☺,☹)							
Length of day's practice session (mins)							
Summary of week's practice time (mins)	Total / Days = Average						

Week 13: Reflection

Date:

Listening / Watching / Reading Notes

Piece / Topic:

Piece / Topic:

Things to work on or be more mindful about

Questions to answer

Positive thoughts and self-criticism

Weekly Check-in

What most inspired you musically or creatively this week?

Which assignment went best for you this week? Why?

What was the hardest part of your practicing this week?

What thought or idea do you want to keep in mind as you commence next week's practice?

| Overall, how satisfied were you with your music practice this week? (1= not at all satisfied, 10 = very satisfied) | ① | ② | ③ | ④ | ⑤ | ⑥ | ⑦ | ⑧ | ⑨ | ⑩ |

Date: Day of the week

Warm-up / Preparation

	reps/mins	○	○	○	○	○	○	○
	reps/mins	○	○	○	○	○	○	○
	reps/mins	○	○	○	○	○	○	○
	reps/mins	○	○	○	○	○	○	○
	reps/mins	○	○	○	○	○	○	○

Exploration / Improvisation / Discovery

	mins	○	○	○	○	○	○	○
	mins	○	○	○	○	○	○	○
	mins	○	○	○	○	○	○	○

Fundamentals / Drills

	reps/mins	○	○	○	○	○	○	○
	reps/mins	○	○	○	○	○	○	○
	reps/mins	○	○	○	○	○	○	○
	reps/mins	○	○	○	○	○	○	○
	reps/mins	○	○	○	○	○	○	○
	reps/mins	○	○	○	○	○	○	○
	reps/mins	○	○	○	○	○	○	○

Week's Focus

	reps/mins	○	○	○	○	○	○	○
	reps/mins	○	○	○	○	○	○	○
	reps/mins	○	○	○	○	○	○	○
	reps/mins	○	○	○	○	○	○	○
	reps/mins	○	○	○	○	○	○	○
	reps/mins	○	○	○	○	○	○	○
	reps/mins	○	○	○	○	○	○	○

Repertoire / Review / Rehearsal

	reps/mins	○	○	○	○	○	○	○
	reps/mins	○	○	○	○	○	○	○
	reps/mins	○	○	○	○	○	○	○
	reps/mins	○	○	○	○	○	○	○
	reps/mins	○	○	○	○	○	○	○

Daily Summary

Practice session quality (rate ☺,☻,☹)							
Length of day's practice session (mins)							
Summary of week's practice time (mins)	Total / Days = Average

Week 14: Reflection

Date:

Listening / Watching / Reading Notes

Piece / Topic:

Piece / Topic:

Things to work on or be more mindful about

Questions to answer

Positive thoughts and self-criticism

Weekly Check-in

What most inspired you musically or creatively this week?

Which assignment went best for you this week? Why?

What was the hardest part of your practicing this week?

What thought or idea do you want to keep in mind as you commence next week's practice?

| Overall, how satisfied were you with your music practice this week? (1= not at all satisfied, 10 = very satisfied) | ① | ② | ③ | ④ | ⑤ | ⑥ | ⑦ | ⑧ | ⑨ | ⑩ |

Date: Day of the week

Warm-up / Preparation

	reps/mins	○ ○ ○ ○ ○ ○ ○
	reps/mins	○ ○ ○ ○ ○ ○ ○
	reps/mins	○ ○ ○ ○ ○ ○ ○
	reps/mins	○ ○ ○ ○ ○ ○ ○
	reps/mins	○ ○ ○ ○ ○ ○ ○

Exploration / Improvisation / Discovery

	mins	○ ○ ○ ○ ○ ○ ○
	mins	○ ○ ○ ○ ○ ○ ○
	mins	○ ○ ○ ○ ○ ○ ○

Fundamentals / Drills

	reps/mins	○ ○ ○ ○ ○ ○ ○
	reps/mins	○ ○ ○ ○ ○ ○ ○
	reps/mins	○ ○ ○ ○ ○ ○ ○
	reps/mins	○ ○ ○ ○ ○ ○ ○
	reps/mins	○ ○ ○ ○ ○ ○ ○
	reps/mins	○ ○ ○ ○ ○ ○ ○
	reps/mins	○ ○ ○ ○ ○ ○ ○

Week's Focus

	reps/mins	○ ○ ○ ○ ○ ○ ○
	reps/mins	○ ○ ○ ○ ○ ○ ○
	reps/mins	○ ○ ○ ○ ○ ○ ○
	reps/mins	○ ○ ○ ○ ○ ○ ○
	reps/mins	○ ○ ○ ○ ○ ○ ○
	reps/mins	○ ○ ○ ○ ○ ○ ○
	reps/mins	○ ○ ○ ○ ○ ○ ○

Repertoire / Review / Rehearsal

	reps/mins	○ ○ ○ ○ ○ ○ ○
	reps/mins	○ ○ ○ ○ ○ ○ ○
	reps/mins	○ ○ ○ ○ ○ ○ ○
	reps/mins	○ ○ ○ ○ ○ ○ ○
	reps/mins	○ ○ ○ ○ ○ ○ ○

Daily Summary

Practice session quality (rate ☺,☺,☹)
Length of day's practice session (mins)
Summary of week's practice time (mins)   Total / Days = Average

43

Week 15: Reflection

Date:

Listening / Watching / Reading Notes

Piece / Topic:	Piece / Topic:

Things to work on or be more mindful about

Questions to answer

Positive thoughts and self-criticism

Weekly Check-in

What most inspired you musically or creatively this week?

Which assignment went best for you this week? Why?

What was the hardest part of your practicing this week?

What thought or idea do you want to keep in mind as you commence next week's practice?

Overall, how satisfied were you with your music practice this week? (1= not at all satisfied, 10 = very satisfied)   ① ② ③ ④ ⑤ ⑥ ⑦ ⑧ ⑨ ⑩

Date:

Day of the week

Warm-up / Preparation

	reps/mins	○	○	○	○	○	○	○
	reps/mins	○	○	○	○	○	○	○
	reps/mins	○	○	○	○	○	○	○
	reps/mins	○	○	○	○	○	○	○
	reps/mins	○	○	○	○	○	○	○

Exploration / Improvisation / Discovery

	mins	○	○	○	○	○	○	○
	mins	○	○	○	○	○	○	○
	mins	○	○	○	○	○	○	○

Fundamentals / Drills

	reps/mins	○	○	○	○	○	○	○
	reps/mins	○	○	○	○	○	○	○
	reps/mins	○	○	○	○	○	○	○
	reps/mins	○	○	○	○	○	○	○
	reps/mins	○	○	○	○	○	○	○
	reps/mins	○	○	○	○	○	○	○
	reps/mins	○	○	○	○	○	○	○

Week's Focus

	reps/mins	○	○	○	○	○	○	○
	reps/mins	○	○	○	○	○	○	○
	reps/mins	○	○	○	○	○	○	○
	reps/mins	○	○	○	○	○	○	○
	reps/mins	○	○	○	○	○	○	○
	reps/mins	○	○	○	○	○	○	○
	reps/mins	○	○	○	○	○	○	○

Repertoire / Review / Rehearsal

	reps/mins	○	○	○	○	○	○	○
	reps/mins	○	○	○	○	○	○	○
	reps/mins	○	○	○	○	○	○	○
	reps/mins	○	○	○	○	○	○	○
	reps/mins	○	○	○	○	○	○	○

Daily Summary

Practice session quality (rate ☺,😐,☹)	
Length of day's practice session (mins)	
Summary of week's practice time (mins)	Total / Days = Average

Week 16: Reflection

Date:

Listening / Watching / Reading Notes

Piece / Topic:

Piece / Topic:

Things to work on or be more mindful about

Questions to answer

Positive thoughts and self-criticism

Weekly Check-in

What most inspired you musically or creatively this week?

Which assignment went best for you this week? Why?

What was the hardest part of your practicing this week?

What thought or idea do you want to keep in mind as you commence next week's practice?

Overall, how satisfied were you with your music practice this week? (1= not at all satisfied, 10 = very satisfied)   ① ② ③ ④ ⑤ ⑥ ⑦ ⑧ ⑨ ⑩

Date: Day of the week

Warm-up / Preparation

	reps/mins	○	○	○	○	○	○	○
	reps/mins	○	○	○	○	○	○	○
	reps/mins	○	○	○	○	○	○	○
	reps/mins	○	○	○	○	○	○	○
	reps/mins	○	○	○	○	○	○	○

Exploration / Improvisation / Discovery

	mins	○	○	○	○	○	○	○
	mins	○	○	○	○	○	○	○
	mins	○	○	○	○	○	○	○

Fundamentals / Drills

	reps/mins	○	○	○	○	○	○	○
	reps/mins	○	○	○	○	○	○	○
	reps/mins	○	○	○	○	○	○	○
	reps/mins	○	○	○	○	○	○	○
	reps/mins	○	○	○	○	○	○	○
	reps/mins	○	○	○	○	○	○	○
	reps/mins	○	○	○	○	○	○	○

Week's Focus

	reps/mins	○	○	○	○	○	○	○
	reps/mins	○	○	○	○	○	○	○
	reps/mins	○	○	○	○	○	○	○
	reps/mins	○	○	○	○	○	○	○
	reps/mins	○	○	○	○	○	○	○
	reps/mins	○	○	○	○	○	○	○
	reps/mins	○	○	○	○	○	○	○

Repertoire / Review / Rehearsal

	reps/mins	○	○	○	○	○	○	○
	reps/mins	○	○	○	○	○	○	○
	reps/mins	○	○	○	○	○	○	○
	reps/mins	○	○	○	○	○	○	○
	reps/mins	○	○	○	○	○	○	○

Daily Summary

Practice session quality (rate ☺,☻,☹)							
Length of day's practice session (mins)							
Summary of week's practice time (mins)	Total /	Days =				Average	

Week 17: Reflection

Date:

Listening / Watching / Reading Notes

Piece / Topic:

Piece / Topic:

Things to work on or be more mindful about

Questions to answer

Positive thoughts and self-criticism

Weekly Check-in

What most inspired you musically or creatively this week?

Which assignment went best for you this week? Why?

What was the hardest part of your practicing this week?

What thought or idea do you want to keep in mind as you commence next week's practice?

Overall, how satisfied were you with your music practice this week? (1= not at all satisfied, 10 = very satisfied) ① ② ③ ④ ⑤ ⑥ ⑦ ⑧ ⑨ ⑩

Date: Day of the week

Warm-up / Preparation

_____ reps/mins	○	○	○	○	○	○	○
_____ reps/mins	○	○	○	○	○	○	○
_____ reps/mins	○	○	○	○	○	○	○
_____ reps/mins	○	○	○	○	○	○	○
_____ reps/mins	○	○	○	○	○	○	○

Exploration / Improvisation / Discovery

_____ mins	○	○	○	○	○	○	○
_____ mins	○	○	○	○	○	○	○
_____ mins	○	○	○	○	○	○	○

Fundamentals / Drills

_____ reps/mins	○	○	○	○	○	○	○
_____ reps/mins	○	○	○	○	○	○	○
_____ reps/mins	○	○	○	○	○	○	○
_____ reps/mins	○	○	○	○	○	○	○
_____ reps/mins	○	○	○	○	○	○	○
_____ reps/mins	○	○	○	○	○	○	○
_____ reps/mins	○	○	○	○	○	○	○

Week's Focus

_____ reps/mins	○	○	○	○	○	○	○
_____ reps/mins	○	○	○	○	○	○	○
_____ reps/mins	○	○	○	○	○	○	○
_____ reps/mins	○	○	○	○	○	○	○
_____ reps/mins	○	○	○	○	○	○	○
_____ reps/mins	○	○	○	○	○	○	○
_____ reps/mins	○	○	○	○	○	○	○

Repertoire / Review / Rehearsal

_____ reps/mins	○	○	○	○	○	○	○
_____ reps/mins	○	○	○	○	○	○	○
_____ reps/mins	○	○	○	○	○	○	○
_____ reps/mins	○	○	○	○	○	○	○
_____ reps/mins	○	○	○	○	○	○	○

Daily Summary

Practice session quality (rate ☺,☺,☹)							
Length of day's practice session (mins)							
Summary of week's practice time (mins)	Total /	Days =			Average		

Week 18: Reflection

Date:

Listening / Watching / Reading Notes

Piece / Topic:	Piece / Topic:

Things to work on or be more mindful about

Questions to answer

Positive thoughts and self-criticism

Weekly Check-in

What most inspired you musically or creatively this week?

Which assignment went best for you this week? Why?

What was the hardest part of your practicing this week?

What thought or idea do you want to keep in mind as you commence next week's practice?

Overall, how satisfied were you with your music practice this week? (1= not at all satisfied, 10 = very satisfied) ① ② ③ ④ ⑤ ⑥ ⑦ ⑧ ⑨ ⑩

Date: Day of the week

Warm-up / Preparation

	reps/mins	○	○	○	○	○	○	○
	reps/mins	○	○	○	○	○	○	○
	reps/mins	○	○	○	○	○	○	○
	reps/mins	○	○	○	○	○	○	○
	reps/mins	○	○	○	○	○	○	○

Exploration / Improvisation / Discovery

	mins	○	○	○	○	○	○	○
	mins	○	○	○	○	○	○	○
	mins	○	○	○	○	○	○	○

Fundamentals / Drills

	reps/mins	○	○	○	○	○	○	○
	reps/mins	○	○	○	○	○	○	○
	reps/mins	○	○	○	○	○	○	○
	reps/mins	○	○	○	○	○	○	○
	reps/mins	○	○	○	○	○	○	○
	reps/mins	○	○	○	○	○	○	○
	reps/mins	○	○	○	○	○	○	○

Week's Focus

	reps/mins	○	○	○	○	○	○	○
	reps/mins	○	○	○	○	○	○	○
	reps/mins	○	○	○	○	○	○	○
	reps/mins	○	○	○	○	○	○	○
	reps/mins	○	○	○	○	○	○	○
	reps/mins	○	○	○	○	○	○	○
	reps/mins	○	○	○	○	○	○	○

Repertoire / Review / Rehearsal

	reps/mins	○	○	○	○	○	○	○
	reps/mins	○	○	○	○	○	○	○
	reps/mins	○	○	○	○	○	○	○
	reps/mins	○	○	○	○	○	○	○
	reps/mins	○	○	○	○	○	○	○

Daily Summary

Practice session quality (rate ☺,☺,☹)							
Length of day's practice session (mins)							
Summary of week's practice time (mins)	Total / Days = Average

Week 19: Reflection

Date:

Listening / Watching / Reading Notes

Piece / Topic:

Piece / Topic:

Things to work on or be more mindful about

Questions to answer

Positive thoughts and self-criticism

Weekly Check-in

What most inspired you musically or creatively this week?

Which assignment went best for you this week? Why?

What was the hardest part of your practicing this week?

What thought or idea do you want to keep in mind as you commence next week's practice?

| Overall, how satisfied were you with your music practice this week? (1= not at all satisfied, 10 = very satisfied) | ① | ② | ③ | ④ | ⑤ | ⑥ | ⑦ | ⑧ | ⑨ | ⑩ |

Date: Day of the week

Warm-up / Preparation

	reps/mins	○	○	○	○	○	○	○
	reps/mins	○	○	○	○	○	○	○
	reps/mins	○	○	○	○	○	○	○
	reps/mins	○	○	○	○	○	○	○
	reps/mins	○	○	○	○	○	○	○

Exploration / Improvisation / Discovery

	mins	○	○	○	○	○	○	○
	mins	○	○	○	○	○	○	○
	mins	○	○	○	○	○	○	○

Fundamentals / Drills

	reps/mins	○	○	○	○	○	○	○
	reps/mins	○	○	○	○	○	○	○
	reps/mins	○	○	○	○	○	○	○
	reps/mins	○	○	○	○	○	○	○
	reps/mins	○	○	○	○	○	○	○
	reps/mins	○	○	○	○	○	○	○
	reps/mins	○	○	○	○	○	○	○

Week's Focus

	reps/mins	○	○	○	○	○	○	○
	reps/mins	○	○	○	○	○	○	○
	reps/mins	○	○	○	○	○	○	○
	reps/mins	○	○	○	○	○	○	○
	reps/mins	○	○	○	○	○	○	○
	reps/mins	○	○	○	○	○	○	○
	reps/mins	○	○	○	○	○	○	○

Repertoire / Review / Rehearsal

	reps/mins	○	○	○	○	○	○	○
	reps/mins	○	○	○	○	○	○	○
	reps/mins	○	○	○	○	○	○	○
	reps/mins	○	○	○	○	○	○	○
	reps/mins	○	○	○	○	○	○	○

Daily Summary

Practice session quality (rate ☺,☺,☹)							
Length of day's practice session (mins)							
Summary of week's practice time (mins)	Total /	Days =			Average		

Week 20: Reflection

Date:

Listening / Watching / Reading Notes

Piece / Topic:

Piece / Topic:

Things to work on or be more mindful about

Questions to answer

Positive thoughts and self-criticism

Weekly Check-in

What most inspired you musically or creatively this week?

Which assignment went best for you this week? Why?

What was the hardest part of your practicing this week?

What thought or idea do you want to keep in mind as you commence next week's practice?

Overall, how satisfied were you with your music practice this week? (1= not at all satisfied, 10 = very satisfied) ① ② ③ ④ ⑤ ⑥ ⑦ ⑧ ⑨ ⑩

Date: Day of the week

Warm-up / Preparation

	reps/mins	◯	◯	◯	◯	◯	◯	◯
	reps/mins	◯	◯	◯	◯	◯	◯	◯
	reps/mins	◯	◯	◯	◯	◯	◯	◯
	reps/mins	◯	◯	◯	◯	◯	◯	◯
	reps/mins	◯	◯	◯	◯	◯	◯	◯

Exploration / Improvisation / Discovery

	mins	◯	◯	◯	◯	◯	◯	◯
	mins	◯	◯	◯	◯	◯	◯	◯
	mins	◯	◯	◯	◯	◯	◯	◯

Fundamentals / Drills

	reps/mins	◯	◯	◯	◯	◯	◯	◯
	reps/mins	◯	◯	◯	◯	◯	◯	◯
	reps/mins	◯	◯	◯	◯	◯	◯	◯
	reps/mins	◯	◯	◯	◯	◯	◯	◯
	reps/mins	◯	◯	◯	◯	◯	◯	◯
	reps/mins	◯	◯	◯	◯	◯	◯	◯
	reps/mins	◯	◯	◯	◯	◯	◯	◯

Week's Focus

	reps/mins	◯	◯	◯	◯	◯	◯	◯
	reps/mins	◯	◯	◯	◯	◯	◯	◯
	reps/mins	◯	◯	◯	◯	◯	◯	◯
	reps/mins	◯	◯	◯	◯	◯	◯	◯
	reps/mins	◯	◯	◯	◯	◯	◯	◯
	reps/mins	◯	◯	◯	◯	◯	◯	◯
	reps/mins	◯	◯	◯	◯	◯	◯	◯

Repertoire / Review / Rehearsal

	reps/mins	◯	◯	◯	◯	◯	◯	◯
	reps/mins	◯	◯	◯	◯	◯	◯	◯
	reps/mins	◯	◯	◯	◯	◯	◯	◯
	reps/mins	◯	◯	◯	◯	◯	◯	◯
	reps/mins	◯	◯	◯	◯	◯	◯	◯

Daily Summary

Practice session quality (rate ☺,😐,☹)	
Length of day's practice session (mins)	
Summary of week's practice time (mins)	Total / Days = Average

Week 21: Reflection

Date:

Listening / Watching / Reading Notes

Piece / Topic:

Piece / Topic:

Things to work on or be more mindful about

Questions to answer

Positive thoughts and self-criticism

Weekly Check-in

What most inspired you musically or creatively this week?

Which assignment went best for you this week? Why?

What was the hardest part of your practicing this week?

What thought or idea do you want to keep in mind as you commence next week's practice?

Overall, how satisfied were you with your music practice this week? (1= not at all satisfied, 10 = very satisfied)	①	②	③	④	⑤	⑥	⑦	⑧	⑨	⑩

Date: _____   Day of the week

Warm-up / Preparation

_____ reps/mins	○	○	○	○	○	○	○
_____ reps/mins	○	○	○	○	○	○	○
_____ reps/mins	○	○	○	○	○	○	○
_____ reps/mins	○	○	○	○	○	○	○
_____ reps/mins	○	○	○	○	○	○	○

Exploration / Improvisation / Discovery

_____ mins	○	○	○	○	○	○	○
_____ mins	○	○	○	○	○	○	○
_____ mins	○	○	○	○	○	○	○

Fundamentals / Drills

_____ reps/mins	○	○	○	○	○	○	○
_____ reps/mins	○	○	○	○	○	○	○
_____ reps/mins	○	○	○	○	○	○	○
_____ reps/mins	○	○	○	○	○	○	○
_____ reps/mins	○	○	○	○	○	○	○
_____ reps/mins	○	○	○	○	○	○	○
_____ reps/mins	○	○	○	○	○	○	○

Week's Focus

_____ reps/mins	○	○	○	○	○	○	○
_____ reps/mins	○	○	○	○	○	○	○
_____ reps/mins	○	○	○	○	○	○	○
_____ reps/mins	○	○	○	○	○	○	○
_____ reps/mins	○	○	○	○	○	○	○
_____ reps/mins	○	○	○	○	○	○	○
_____ reps/mins	○	○	○	○	○	○	○

Repertoire / Review / Rehearsal

_____ reps/mins	○	○	○	○	○	○	○
_____ reps/mins	○	○	○	○	○	○	○
_____ reps/mins	○	○	○	○	○	○	○
_____ reps/mins	○	○	○	○	○	○	○
_____ reps/mins	○	○	○	○	○	○	○

Daily Summary

Practice session quality (rate ☺,☺,☹)							
Length of day's practice session (mins)							
Summary of week's practice time (mins)	Total / Days = Average						

Week 22: Reflection

Date:

Listening / Watching / Reading Notes

Piece / Topic:

Piece / Topic:

Things to work on or be more mindful about

Questions to answer

Positive thoughts and self-criticism

Weekly Check-in

What most inspired you musically or creatively this week?

Which assignment went best for you this week? Why?

What was the hardest part of your practicing this week?

What thought or idea do you want to keep in mind as you commence next week's practice?

| Overall, how satisfied were you with your music practice this week? (1= not at all satisfied, 10 = very satisfied) | ① | ② | ③ | ④ | ⑤ | ⑥ | ⑦ | ⑧ | ⑨ | ⑩ |

Date: Day of the week

Warm-up / Preparation

reps/mins ○ ○ ○ ○ ○ ○ ○
reps/mins ○ ○ ○ ○ ○ ○ ○
reps/mins ○ ○ ○ ○ ○ ○ ○
reps/mins ○ ○ ○ ○ ○ ○ ○
reps/mins ○ ○ ○ ○ ○ ○ ○

Exploration / Improvisation / Discovery

mins ○ ○ ○ ○ ○ ○ ○
mins ○ ○ ○ ○ ○ ○ ○
mins ○ ○ ○ ○ ○ ○ ○

Fundamentals / Drills

reps/mins ○ ○ ○ ○ ○ ○ ○
reps/mins ○ ○ ○ ○ ○ ○ ○
reps/mins ○ ○ ○ ○ ○ ○ ○
reps/mins ○ ○ ○ ○ ○ ○ ○
reps/mins ○ ○ ○ ○ ○ ○ ○
reps/mins ○ ○ ○ ○ ○ ○ ○
reps/mins ○ ○ ○ ○ ○ ○ ○

Week's Focus

reps/mins ○ ○ ○ ○ ○ ○ ○
reps/mins ○ ○ ○ ○ ○ ○ ○
reps/mins ○ ○ ○ ○ ○ ○ ○
reps/mins ○ ○ ○ ○ ○ ○ ○
reps/mins ○ ○ ○ ○ ○ ○ ○
reps/mins ○ ○ ○ ○ ○ ○ ○
reps/mins ○ ○ ○ ○ ○ ○ ○

Repertoire / Review / Rehearsal

reps/mins ○ ○ ○ ○ ○ ○ ○
reps/mins ○ ○ ○ ○ ○ ○ ○
reps/mins ○ ○ ○ ○ ○ ○ ○
reps/mins ○ ○ ○ ○ ○ ○ ○
reps/mins ○ ○ ○ ○ ○ ○ ○

Daily Summary

Practice session quality (rate ☺,☺,☹)							
Length of day's practice session (mins)							
Summary of week's practice time (mins)	Total /	Days =				Average	

Week 23: Reflection

Date:

Listening / Watching / Reading Notes

Piece / Topic:

Piece / Topic:

Things to work on or be more mindful about

Questions to answer

Positive thoughts and self-criticism

Weekly Check-in

What most inspired you musically or creatively this week?

Which assignment went best for you this week? Why?

What was the hardest part of your practicing this week?

What thought or idea do you want to keep in mind as you commence next week's practice?

| Overall, how satisfied were you with your music practice this week? (1= not at all satisfied, 10 = very satisfied) | ① | ② | ③ | ④ | ⑤ | ⑥ | ⑦ | ⑧ | ⑨ | ⑩ |

Date: _____   Day of the week

Warm-up / Preparation

_____	reps/mins	○	○	○	○	○	○	○
_____	reps/mins	○	○	○	○	○	○	○
_____	reps/mins	○	○	○	○	○	○	○
_____	reps/mins	○	○	○	○	○	○	○
_____	reps/mins	○	○	○	○	○	○	○

Exploration / Improvisation / Discovery

_____	mins	○	○	○	○	○	○	○
_____	mins	○	○	○	○	○	○	○
_____	mins	○	○	○	○	○	○	○

Fundamentals / Drills

_____	reps/mins	○	○	○	○	○	○	○
_____	reps/mins	○	○	○	○	○	○	○
_____	reps/mins	○	○	○	○	○	○	○
_____	reps/mins	○	○	○	○	○	○	○
_____	reps/mins	○	○	○	○	○	○	○
_____	reps/mins	○	○	○	○	○	○	○
_____	reps/mins	○	○	○	○	○	○	○

Week's Focus

_____	reps/mins	○	○	○	○	○	○	○
_____	reps/mins	○	○	○	○	○	○	○
_____	reps/mins	○	○	○	○	○	○	○
_____	reps/mins	○	○	○	○	○	○	○
_____	reps/mins	○	○	○	○	○	○	○
_____	reps/mins	○	○	○	○	○	○	○
_____	reps/mins	○	○	○	○	○	○	○

Repertoire / Review / Rehearsal

_____	reps/mins	○	○	○	○	○	○	○
_____	reps/mins	○	○	○	○	○	○	○
_____	reps/mins	○	○	○	○	○	○	○
_____	reps/mins	○	○	○	○	○	○	○
_____	reps/mins	○	○	○	○	○	○	○

Daily Summary

Practice session quality (rate ☺,☺,☹)							
Length of day's practice session (mins)							
Summary of week's practice time (mins)	Total / Days = Average						

Week 24: Reflection

Date:

Listening / Watching / Reading Notes

Piece / Topic:

Piece / Topic:

Things to work on or be more mindful about

Questions to answer

Positive thoughts and self-criticism

Weekly Check-in

What most inspired you musically or creatively this week?

Which assignment went best for you this week? Why?

What was the hardest part of your practicing this week?

What thought or idea do you want to keep in mind as you commence next week's practice?

Overall, how satisfied were you with your music practice this week? (1= not at all satisfied, 10 = very satisfied) ① ② ③ ④ ⑤ ⑥ ⑦ ⑧ ⑨ ⑩

Date: _____ Day of the week

Warm-up / Preparation

	reps/mins	○	○	○	○	○	○	○
	reps/mins	○	○	○	○	○	○	○
	reps/mins	○	○	○	○	○	○	○
	reps/mins	○	○	○	○	○	○	○
	reps/mins	○	○	○	○	○	○	○

Exploration / Improvisation / Discovery

	mins	○	○	○	○	○	○	○
	mins	○	○	○	○	○	○	○
	mins	○	○	○	○	○	○	○

Fundamentals / Drills

	reps/mins	○	○	○	○	○	○	○
	reps/mins	○	○	○	○	○	○	○
	reps/mins	○	○	○	○	○	○	○
	reps/mins	○	○	○	○	○	○	○
	reps/mins	○	○	○	○	○	○	○
	reps/mins	○	○	○	○	○	○	○
	reps/mins	○	○	○	○	○	○	○

Week's Focus

	reps/mins	○	○	○	○	○	○	○
	reps/mins	○	○	○	○	○	○	○
	reps/mins	○	○	○	○	○	○	○
	reps/mins	○	○	○	○	○	○	○
	reps/mins	○	○	○	○	○	○	○
	reps/mins	○	○	○	○	○	○	○
	reps/mins	○	○	○	○	○	○	○

Repertoire / Review / Rehearsal

	reps/mins	○	○	○	○	○	○	○
	reps/mins	○	○	○	○	○	○	○
	reps/mins	○	○	○	○	○	○	○
	reps/mins	○	○	○	○	○	○	○
	reps/mins	○	○	○	○	○	○	○

Daily Summary

Practice session quality (rate ☺,☺,☹)							
Length of day's practice session (mins)							
Summary of week's practice time (mins)	Total / Days = Average						

Week 25: Reflection

Date:

Listening / Watching / Reading Notes

Piece / Topic:

Piece / Topic:

Things to work on or be more mindful about

Questions to answer

Positive thoughts and self-criticism

Weekly Check-in

What most inspired you musically or creatively this week?

Which assignment went best for you this week? Why?

What was the hardest part of your practicing this week?

What thought or idea do you want to keep in mind as you commence next week's practice?

Overall, how satisfied were you with your music practice this week? (1= not at all satisfied, 10 = very satisfied)   ① ② ③ ④ ⑤ ⑥ ⑦ ⑧ ⑨ ⑩

Date: Day of the week

Warm-up / Preparation

_____ reps/mins	○	○	○	○	○	○	○
_____ reps/mins	○	○	○	○	○	○	○
_____ reps/mins	○	○	○	○	○	○	○
_____ reps/mins	○	○	○	○	○	○	○
_____ reps/mins	○	○	○	○	○	○	○

Exploration / Improvisation / Discovery

_____ mins	○	○	○	○	○	○	○
_____ mins	○	○	○	○	○	○	○
_____ mins	○	○	○	○	○	○	○

Fundamentals / Drills

_____ reps/mins	○	○	○	○	○	○	○
_____ reps/mins	○	○	○	○	○	○	○
_____ reps/mins	○	○	○	○	○	○	○
_____ reps/mins	○	○	○	○	○	○	○
_____ reps/mins	○	○	○	○	○	○	○
_____ reps/mins	○	○	○	○	○	○	○
_____ reps/mins	○	○	○	○	○	○	○

Week's Focus

_____ reps/mins	○	○	○	○	○	○	○
_____ reps/mins	○	○	○	○	○	○	○
_____ reps/mins	○	○	○	○	○	○	○
_____ reps/mins	○	○	○	○	○	○	○
_____ reps/mins	○	○	○	○	○	○	○
_____ reps/mins	○	○	○	○	○	○	○
_____ reps/mins	○	○	○	○	○	○	○

Repertoire / Review / Rehearsal

_____ reps/mins	○	○	○	○	○	○	○
_____ reps/mins	○	○	○	○	○	○	○
_____ reps/mins	○	○	○	○	○	○	○
_____ reps/mins	○	○	○	○	○	○	○
_____ reps/mins	○	○	○	○	○	○	○

Daily Summary

Practice session quality (rate ☺,☺,☹)							
Length of day's practice session (mins)							
Summary of week's practice time (mins)	Total /	Days =				Average	

Week 26: Reflection

Date:

Listening / Watching / Reading Notes

Piece / Topic:

Piece / Topic:

Things to work on or be more mindful about

Questions to answer

Positive thoughts and self-criticism

Weekly Check-in

What most inspired you musically or creatively this week?

Which assignment went best for you this week? Why?

What was the hardest part of your practicing this week?

What thought or idea do you want to keep in mind as you commence next week's practice?

| Overall, how satisfied were you with your music practice this week? (1= not at all satisfied, 10 = very satisfied) | ① | ② | ③ | ④ | ⑤ | ⑥ | ⑦ | ⑧ | ⑨ | ⑩ |

Date:

Day of the week

Warm-up / Preparation

	reps/mins	○	○	○	○	○	○	○
	reps/mins	○	○	○	○	○	○	○
	reps/mins	○	○	○	○	○	○	○
	reps/mins	○	○	○	○	○	○	○
	reps/mins	○	○	○	○	○	○	○

Exploration / Improvisation / Discovery

	mins	○	○	○	○	○	○	○
	mins	○	○	○	○	○	○	○
	mins	○	○	○	○	○	○	○

Fundamentals / Drills

	reps/mins	○	○	○	○	○	○	○
	reps/mins	○	○	○	○	○	○	○
	reps/mins	○	○	○	○	○	○	○
	reps/mins	○	○	○	○	○	○	○
	reps/mins	○	○	○	○	○	○	○
	reps/mins	○	○	○	○	○	○	○
	reps/mins	○	○	○	○	○	○	○

Week's Focus

	reps/mins	○	○	○	○	○	○	○
	reps/mins	○	○	○	○	○	○	○
	reps/mins	○	○	○	○	○	○	○
	reps/mins	○	○	○	○	○	○	○
	reps/mins	○	○	○	○	○	○	○
	reps/mins	○	○	○	○	○	○	○
	reps/mins	○	○	○	○	○	○	○

Repertoire / Review / Rehearsal

	reps/mins	○	○	○	○	○	○	○
	reps/mins	○	○	○	○	○	○	○
	reps/mins	○	○	○	○	○	○	○
	reps/mins	○	○	○	○	○	○	○
	reps/mins	○	○	○	○	○	○	○

Daily Summary

Practice session quality (rate ☺,☺,☹)

Length of day's practice session (mins)

Summary of week's practice time (mins)   Total / Days = Average

67

Progress Charts

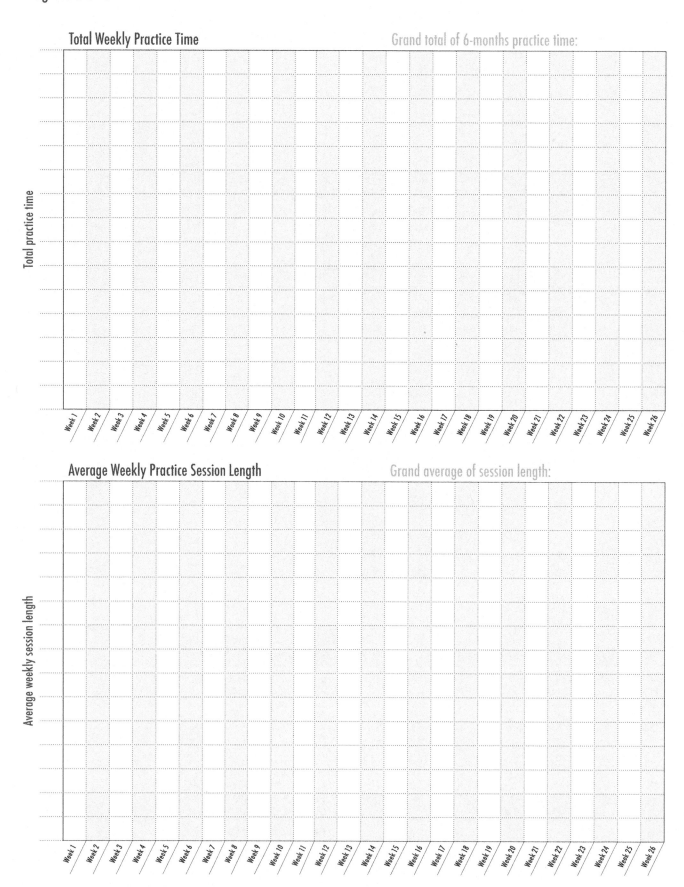

Total Weekly Practice Time

Grand total of 6-months practice time:

Total practice time

Week 1 Week 2 Week 3 Week 4 Week 5 Week 6 Week 7 Week 8 Week 9 Week 10 Week 11 Week 12 Week 13 Week 14 Week 15 Week 16 Week 17 Week 18 Week 19 Week 20 Week 21 Week 22 Week 23 Week 24 Week 25 Week 26

Average Weekly Practice Session Length

Grand average of session length:

Average weekly session length

Week 1 Week 2 Week 3 Week 4 Week 5 Week 6 Week 7 Week 8 Week 9 Week 10 Week 11 Week 12 Week 13 Week 14 Week 15 Week 16 Week 17 Week 18 Week 19 Week 20 Week 21 Week 22 Week 23 Week 24 Week 25 Week 26

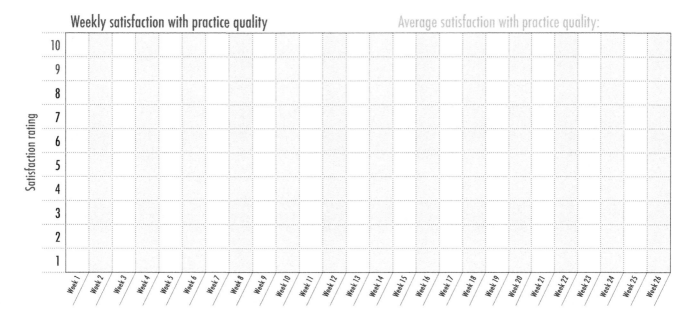

Weekly satisfaction with practice quality

Average satisfaction with practice quality:

Satisfaction rating

10
9
8
7
6
5
4
3
2
1

Week 1 Week 2 Week 3 Week 4 Week 5 Week 6 Week 7 Week 8 Week 9 Week 10 Week 11 Week 12 Week 13 Week 14 Week 15 Week 16 Week 17 Week 18 Week 19 Week 20 Week 21 Week 22 Week 23 Week 24 Week 25 Week 26

Notes and Observations

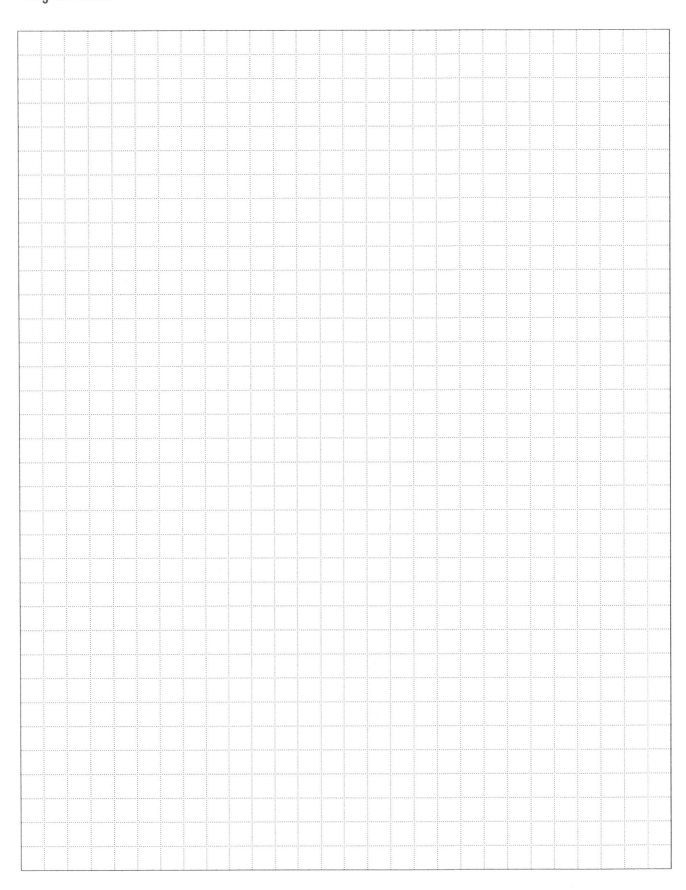

Tips and Exercise Notes

Exercise:

Source:

Exercise:

Source:

Exercise:

Source:

Exercise:

Source:

Exercise:

Source:

Exercise:

Source:

Tips and Exercise Notes

Exercise:

Source:

Exercise:

Source:

Exercise:

Source:

Exercise:

Source:

Exercise:

Source:

Exercise:

Source:

Tips and Exercise Notes

Exercise:

Source:

Exercise:

Source:

Exercise:

Source:

Exercise:

Source:

Exercise:

Source:

Exercise:

Source:

Tips and Exercise Notes

Exercise:

Source:

Exercise:

Source:

Exercise:

Source:

Exercise:

Source:

Exercise:

Source:

Exercise:

Source:

Tips and Exercise Notes

Exercise:

Source:

Exercise:

Source:

Exercise:

Source:

Exercise:

Source:

Exercise:

Source:

Exercise:

Source:

Tips and Exercise Notes

Exercise:

Source:

Exercise:

Source:

Exercise:

Source:

Exercise:

Source:

Exercise:

Source:

Exercise:

Source:

Listening Notes

Piece:

Artist:

Date:

Piece:

Artist:

Date:

Piece:

Artist:

Date:

Piece:

Artist:

Date:

Listening Notes

Piece:

Artist:

Date:

Piece:

Artist:

Date:

Piece:

Artist:

Date:

Piece:

Artist:

Date:

Listening Notes

Piece:

Artist:

Date:

Piece:

Artist:

Date:

Piece:

Artist:

Date:

Piece:

Artist:

Date:

Listening Notes

Piece:

Artist:

Date:

Piece:

Artist:

Date:

Piece:

Artist:

Date:

Piece:

Artist:

Date:

Listening Notes

Piece:

Artist:

Date:

Piece:

Artist:

Date:

Piece:

Artist:

Date:

Piece:

Artist:

Date:

Listening Notes

Piece:

Artist:

Date:

Piece:

Artist:

Date:

Piece:

Artist:

Date:

Piece:

Artist:

Date:

Thoughts and Meditations

Thoughts and Meditations

Thoughts and Meditations

6-month Reflection and The Path Forward

What single musical accomplishment made you the proudest?

What other musical accomplishments also made you very proud?

What personal insights and observations arose during your past six months of practice?

What musical or creative inspiration over the past six months stands out the most?

What were your most common obstacles to practice?

What did you tend to tell yourself when you were self-critical, didn't practice, or avoided practice?

What is the evidence that those thoughts are true?

What would you tell a best friend who was having similar thoughts?

What bothers you about the way your practices over the past six months had happened?

What would happen if you didn't change a thing about how you practice?

How would you like for practice to be different?

What would you be willing to try?

What would be the advantages of changing your practice in those ways?

What is going to have to be different to make that change happen?

What encourages you that you could practice differently and better if you wanted to?

What or who could provide you with helpful support in getting started and sticking with it?

Thinking back on the past six months, for what are you most grateful?

What single positive word, phrase, or thought do you want to guide your next six months of practice?

Repertoire

Title

Plus sign for week added to repertoire; circle or check weeks on which included in Weekly Practice Journal

Title	1	2	3	4	5	6	7	8	9	10	11	12	13	14	15	16	17	18	19	20	21	22	23	24	25	26
	1	2	3	4	5	6	7	8	9	10	11	12	13	14	15	16	17	18	19	20	21	22	23	24	25	26
	1	2	3	4	5	6	7	8	9	10	11	12	13	14	15	16	17	18	19	20	21	22	23	24	25	26
	1	2	3	4	5	6	7	8	9	10	11	12	13	14	15	16	17	18	19	20	21	22	23	24	25	26
	1	2	3	4	5	6	7	8	9	10	11	12	13	14	15	16	17	18	19	20	21	22	23	24	25	26
	1	2	3	4	5	6	7	8	9	10	11	12	13	14	15	16	17	18	19	20	21	22	23	24	25	26
	1	2	3	4	5	6	7	8	9	10	11	12	13	14	15	16	17	18	19	20	21	22	23	24	25	26
	1	2	3	4	5	6	7	8	9	10	11	12	13	14	15	16	17	18	19	20	21	22	23	24	25	26
	1	2	3	4	5	6	7	8	9	10	11	12	13	14	15	16	17	18	19	20	21	22	23	24	25	26
	1	2	3	4	5	6	7	8	9	10	11	12	13	14	15	16	17	18	19	20	21	22	23	24	25	26
	1	2	3	4	5	6	7	8	9	10	11	12	13	14	15	16	17	18	19	20	21	22	23	24	25	26
	1	2	3	4	5	6	7	8	9	10	11	12	13	14	15	16	17	18	19	20	21	22	23	24	25	26
	1	2	3	4	5	6	7	8	9	10	11	12	13	14	15	16	17	18	19	20	21	22	23	24	25	26
	1	2	3	4	5	6	7	8	9	10	11	12	13	14	15	16	17	18	19	20	21	22	23	24	25	26
	1	2	3	4	5	6	7	8	9	10	11	12	13	14	15	16	17	18	19	20	21	22	23	24	25	26
	1	2	3	4	5	6	7	8	9	10	11	12	13	14	15	16	17	18	19	20	21	22	23	24	25	26
	1	2	3	4	5	6	7	8	9	10	11	12	13	14	15	16	17	18	19	20	21	22	23	24	25	26
	1	2	3	4	5	6	7	8	9	10	11	12	13	14	15	16	17	18	19	20	21	22	23	24	25	26
	1	2	3	4	5	6	7	8	9	10	11	12	13	14	15	16	17	18	19	20	21	22	23	24	25	26
	1	2	3	4	5	6	7	8	9	10	11	12	13	14	15	16	17	18	19	20	21	22	23	24	25	26
	1	2	3	4	5	6	7	8	9	10	11	12	13	14	15	16	17	18	19	20	21	22	23	24	25	26
	1	2	3	4	5	6	7	8	9	10	11	12	13	14	15	16	17	18	19	20	21	22	23	24	25	26
	1	2	3	4	5	6	7	8	9	10	11	12	13	14	15	16	17	18	19	20	21	22	23	24	25	26
	1	2	3	4	5	6	7	8	9	10	11	12	13	14	15	16	17	18	19	20	21	22	23	24	25	26
	1	2	3	4	5	6	7	8	9	10	11	12	13	14	15	16	17	18	19	20	21	22	23	24	25	26
	1	2	3	4	5	6	7	8	9	10	11	12	13	14	15	16	17	18	19	20	21	22	23	24	25	26
	1	2	3	4	5	6	7	8	9	10	11	12	13	14	15	16	17	18	19	20	21	22	23	24	25	26
	1	2	3	4	5	6	7	8	9	10	11	12	13	14	15	16	17	18	19	20	21	22	23	24	25	26
	1	2	3	4	5	6	7	8	9	10	11	12	13	14	15	16	17	18	19	20	21	22	23	24	25	26

Made in the USA
Coppell, TX
22 April 2022

76919968R00057